Sharing Wisdom

Interreligious Reflections

Series Editor
Alon Goshen-Gottstein, director, Elijah Interfaith Institute

With the rise of interfaith relations comes the challenge of providing theory and deeper understanding for these relations and the trials that religions face together in an increasingly globalized word. Interreligious Reflections addresses these challenges by offering collaborative volumes that reflect cycles of work undertaken in dialogue between scholars of different religions. The series is dedicated to the academic and theological work of The Elijah Interfaith Institute, a multinational organization dedicated to fostering peace between the world's diverse faith communities through interfaith dialogue, education, research, and dissemination. In carrying out Elijah's principles, these volumes extend beyond the Abrahamic paradigm to include the dharmic traditions. As such, they promise to be a source of continuing inspiration and interest for religious leaders, academics, and communitiy-oriented study groups that seek to deepen their interfaith engagement. All volumes in this series are edited by Elijah's director Dr. Alon Goshen-Gottstein.

Titles in the Series

The Religious Other: Hostility, Hospitatlity, and the Hope of Human Flourishing, edited by Alon Goshen-Gottstein

The Crisis of the Holy: Challenges and Transformations in World Religions, edited by Alon Goshen-Gottstein

Friendship across Religions: Theological Perspectives on Interreligious Friendship, edited by Alon Goshen-Gottstein

Memory and Hope: Forgiveness, Healing, and Interfaith Relations, edited by Alon Goshen-Gottstein

The Future of Religous Leadership: World Religions in Coversations, edited by Alon Goshen-Gottstein

Sharing Wisdom: Benefits and Boundaries of Interreligious Learning, edited by Alon Goshen-Gottstein

Sharing Wisdom

*Benefits and Boundaries
of Interreligious Learning*

Edited by Alon Goshen-Gottstein

WIPF & STOCK · Eugene, Oregon

Wipf and Stock Publishers
199 W 8th Ave, Suite 3
Eugene, OR 97401

Sharing Wisdom
Benefits and Boundaries of Interreligious Learning
By Goshen-Gottstein, Alon
Copyright©2017 Rowman and Littlefield Publishing Group
ISBN 13: 978-1-5326-5924-9
Publication date 5/25/2018
Previously published by Lexington Books, 2017

For Barry and Connie Hershey
Lovers of wisdom, wherever it is found

Contents

Foreword		ix
	Alon Goshen-Gottstein	
Introduction: Sharing Wisdom		xi
	Alon Goshen-Gottstein	
1	A Christian Perspective	1
	Miroslav Volf	
2	A Hindu Perspective	19
	Anantanand Rambachan	
3	A Sikh Perspective	33
	Pal Ahluwalia	
4	A Buddhist Perspective	45
	Sallie B. King	
5	A Muslim Perspective	61
	Timothy J. Gianotti	
6	A Jewish Perspective	79
	Meir Sendor	
7	Sharing Wisdom: A Composite Picture	95
	Alon Goshen-Gottstein	
Bibliography		113
Index		115
About the Contributors		117

Foreword

Alon Goshen-Gottstein

It is with great pleasure that we present the sixth volume in the *Interreligious Reflections* series. The discussions in this volume go to the heart of the concerns of this series—what it means to be engaging the world of thought and belief of other religions and how sharing of wisdom between religious traditions can enhance relationships between them, the self-understanding of each, the common voice that religions are to have in the world and the spiritual quest that is common to all faith traditions.

The chapters were written initially for the third meeting of the Elijah Board of World Religious Leaders, that was hosted by His Holiness the Dalai Lama and by Bhai Sahib Bhai Mohinder Singh in Amritsar, in 2007. They have been updated for purposes of the present publication.[1]

The Amritsar meeting benefited from the support of several foundations. I recall with gratitude the support of the Von Groeben Foundation as well as the Udo Keller Foundation. The work on Sharing Wisdom was supported in the main by the Fetzer Institute. Our group of scholars held two in person meetings at Fetzer's facilities in Kalamazoo. The Fetzer vision finds expression in these chapters in the focus on love and forgiveness as expressions of sharing wisdom. Fetzer warmth and hospitality can only be expressed between the lines, but remains engraved in the memory of all participants. Eric Nelson and David Addiss, who represented Fetzer at that meeting, were deeply engaged in our discussions and contributed much to them.

The primary contributors to the project are the scholars whose work is featured in this volume. They were not the only ones. I recall with gratitude the contributions of several scholars to our conversations. These include (in alphabetical order) Therese Andrevon, Barry Levy, Vanessa Sasson, Kurt Schreiber and Johann Vento. Working together bonded us as a group and the power of those relationships carries over from one project to the next.

The meetings in Kalamazoo and Amritsar are the subject of a short film that was produced on the work of the think tank and of the Elijah Board of World Religious Leaders. Readers of the present volume that are interested in the accompanying visuals and testimonies, are welcome to view these at http://elijah-interfaith.org/video/dialogue-kalamazoo-and-amritsar-meetings.

Preparation of this manuscript for publication relied extensively on the engaged efforts of Peta Pellach Jones and of Natalee Cohen. Both have shown exceptional talent and patience in bringing this publication to the finish line.

Thanks go to Lexington Books staff. First and foremost, I am grateful to our editor, Sarah Craig, whose competence and professionalism are outstanding. Bethany Davis has been helpful in the day to day. To both of them and to the management of Lexington Books's staff, thank you for your continued vote of confidence in our work.

Let me conclude with the words that served me to conclude my welcome words to the religious leaders gathered in Amritsar. They serve equally to welcome readers to our process of reflection:

> Let Wisdom flourish! Let Peace prevail!

NOTE

1. Only one of them was published elsewhere by its author in the intervening period. The present version offers in the notes reference to relevant texts, not included in the Brazos version.

Introduction

Sharing Wisdom

Alon Goshen-Gottstein

DEFINING THE QUESTIONS

The present project was born, so to speak, in response to a challenge posed by one of the members of the Elijah Board of World Religious Leaders. Sri Sri Ravi Sankar made a statement at a conference jointly attended, in which he posed the following question: "If we can share each other's food, listen to each other's music, and wear each other's clothes, why can we not share each other's wisdom?" This rhetorical question was followed by a call to scholars of different religions to reflect upon the boundaries and strategies for appropriate sharing of wisdom between religious traditions. This challenge goes to the heart of Elijah's work and the present volume seeks to address the challenge.

Some topics have a history of research and reflection upon which they can draw. In working through the present challenge it seemed like we were traversing virgin ground. The reality of conscious and intentional sharing of wisdom between faith traditions as a kind of desideratum, even an ideal, as distinct from the reality of mutual influence on the ground, is a new reality. With this new reality a series of questions opens up, and these questions have served as guides for the present project. The work of the think tank featured in this volume sought to identify key questions that need to be articulated as part of the project and to offer the complementary perspectives of participating religious traditions to these questions. Accordingly, the chapters seek to follow the same format, addressing each of these questions from the perspective of each of the traditions.

The first question that must be addressed is "what is wisdom." We cannot take for granted that there is one understanding of wisdom that is common to the religions, nor the existence of some neutral "third-party" working definition of wisdom. As a condition for understanding how each tradition responds to the questions associated with sharing wisdom, we must begin with an understanding of each tradition's definition, view and approach to wisdom.

The project of sharing wisdom is also not to be taken for granted. Even if sharing wisdom is desirable from a contemporary perspective, we must construct an argument, based upon the religious concerns of each of the traditions, for why, on internal religious grounds, wisdom should be shared across traditions.

Next comes the question of how to share. What are conditions, methods, and emphases that govern an ideal process of sharing wisdom? What internal guidelines may be obtained from the traditions to facilitate sharing across religions, whether these were articulated in the first instance in relation to an audience outside the religion, or whether these were first articulated for internal purposes?

Sharing must be undertaken in a way that is responsible, both to the tradition and to the recipient of wisdom. What are responsible ways of sharing, and related—what are irresponsible ways of sharing and what are pitfalls and dangers that should be avoided? Thus, an ethos for responsible sharing should be articulated for each of the traditions, and eventually for the very project of sharing wisdom across religious traditions.

From these general considerations we move to specific examples. Historically religions have shared with each other. Ideally, religious thinkers may consider there is wisdom in their traditions that should be communicated across religions. Each of our contributors seeks to articulate what is the wisdom in his or her tradition that either has been or should be communicated to others, in other words: the wisdom value that the particular tradition considers to be of enduring significance beyond the particular religion. Similarly, each of the traditions has also received wisdom from others. What are instances of such reception? Clearly, a strong precedent of reception provides legitimation for the very project of sharing wisdom across religions.

Finally, we explore how our religions can bring their wisdom to one particular topic—love and forgiveness. Moving then from the most abstract reflection to a common point of reference, we review what wisdom each of our traditions has to offer on the theme of love and forgiveness. In several instances the theoretical view is complemented by sharing a story or case where these principles have been enacted in recent memory.

The format of a collaborative project of a think tank allows us to work through these issues religion by religion. Our process has benefited from having worked through these issues together and from being inspired by one another's contributions. Each of the chapters delivers its unique message. I will offer my own synthetic overview of the project in its entirety after the reader has had the opportunity of studying the individual chapters. I would, however, like to raise at this point one or two reflections concerning the very nature of the present project.

SHARING WISDOM AND INTERRELIGIOUS DIALOGUE

Let us consider how "Sharing Wisdom" is similar to or different from interreligious dialogue and collaboration? What is the uniqueness of our emphasis upon "Sharing Wisdom?" My own answer would be that "Sharing Wisdom" is the heart of interreligious dialogue. Interreligious dialogue as practiced often brings members of different faith communities together in a show of similarity, or even of difference, that highlights the goodwill and desire for harmony and positive contribution to society that are the driving force behind coming together in the first instance. All too often, the coming together lacks reflectivity and does not draw in meaningful ways from the wellsprings of the traditions themselves. Without detracting from the social and political significance of such coming together, from the religious perspective it is found lacking inasmuch as it does not engage the religious traditions deeply in their own language. One expression of this lack is the double talk and the discrepancy found between statements made to members of one's own faith community and statements made when facing outwards. Meaningful engagement with the religious other is at the same time also an opportunity for deeper engagement with oneself. It is here that we enter wisdom's domain.

As will emerge from our chapters, such a twofold movement can take various forms. The engagement with the other could be a means for stimulating self-critical reflection[1] or a clearer, perhaps novel, articulation of one's own tradition.[2] It could help remind us of an overlooked or forgotten part of our own tradition. It could stimulate us to discover new resources within our traditions to match up to ideals that our tradition had not previously entertained.[3] And it could simply make us more profoundly aware of humanity, in its diversity, expressed in the broad range of religious experience, both similar and different, that we encounter as we encounter practitioners of other religions. However we conceive of the deeper benefits of interreligious engagement, all these aspects point to the wisdom of traditions and rely upon them. All these aspects are also transformative. They lead to a transformation of our vision of ourselves and the other. Such transformation is only possible when wisdom has touched us and we are called to reconsider our view of ourselves and the other in its light. Thus, interreligious dialogue that does not lead to genuine transformation of some kind lacks the touch of wisdom. Sharing wisdom is by its nature transformative.

But wisdom need not be limited to the sharing of ideas and the growth of understanding. Wisdom is also a call to action. As Pal Ahluwalia makes clear in the case of Sikhism, practice and service are two keys to the acquisition and expression of wisdom.[4] As Miroslav Volf suggests, wisdom is a reality that seeks expression.[5] Its expression is in the minds and hearts of those who make a dwelling place for it. But it is also in the action that manifests wisdom and that seeks to make the entire world wisdom's arena of manifestation. Hence, wisdom is a powerful driver for common action. Our chapters bring some potent examples of the call to action growing from the inspiration of sharing wisdom. Thus, Sallie King mentions several instances in which Buddhist teachers were inspired by the wisdom teachings of Christianity to social action as an expression of their Buddhist identity.[6] Similarly Anant Rambachan finds inspiration in both Christian and Buddhist resources, as he reflects upon how to draw Hinduism's own wisdom from the theoretical plane to the level of social reality.[7]

SHARING COMMONALITIES AND DIFFERENCES

The importance we attach to the sharing of wisdom will determine what aspects of our tradition come under the mandate of sharing. It would seem, however, that if we seek to understand humanity in its fullness, nothing should be excluded from the purview of wisdom. Differences will remain. Sharing wisdom, as I understand it, is not a mechanism for obliterating differences. Honest sharing could, however, allow us to discover the depth of humanity, even as it finds expression in that which is different, in the depth of the particular.

From another perspective, sharing wisdom is particularly vital in relation to our differences, rather than to our commonalities. If we highlight only commonalities, then we are not really learning about the other. We are simply uncovering the common ground that we already recognize. In other words, we recognize the other as a form of ourselves. Sharing otherness allows us to recognize multiple expressions of wisdom, even as they assume expressions that are foreign to us. We may choose to do so because we seek a fuller understanding of humanity or because we are open to a broader understanding of what might constitute wisdom. In this context it is worth recalling the observation by Anant Rambachan that meaningful sharing is founded upon the recognition that another tradition can be genuinely enriching.[8] Such recognition is already a form of recognizing some aspect of validity within that tradition. Sharing thus emerges as a strategy for recognition. It may, quite possibly, also be the pedagogy, by means of which we educate others to the acceptance and recognition of other traditions.

A COMMON VOICE, A COMMON VISION

It has been a privilege to think through the issues spelled out above with a group of world class scholar-practitioners, each of whom has thought these issues through from the perspective of his or her tradition. In coming together we sought to not only offer answers to the questions spelled out above from the perspective of the individual tradition. We also sought to make the project of sharing wisdom one that all religions could subscribe to and one that could offer a vision for religious communities. To that end, it was important for us to identify commonalities not only in terms of the project's thematics. These will be teased out in my concluding chapter. It was important for us to identify the project's message as one of contemporary religious and social relevance, as a vision for those who engage in interreligious relations and for religious communities as a whole. To that end, we attempted to articulate what the project has taught us through a series of affirmations or recognitions that sum up for all of us what this project has been about. These affirmations can serve not only as a summary of the project but also as an invitation for others to enter into the domain of sharing wisdom.[9] Set at the introduction to the present book, they offer a frame of meaning for the individual chapters.

THE SPIRIT OF SHARING WISDOM

The Need

- We are profoundly aware of the many needs, pains, and crises in the world and within our own religious traditions.
- We are aware of the violence engendered by practitioners of different religious traditions towards practitioners of other religions. We note with sadness that such violence is often the outcome of misinformation, lack of understanding of the other, demonization and dehumanization of the other.
- We are aware that our image of members of other faith traditions often lacks respect, leading to sacrilege and abuse of religious symbols of other traditions. We note that this too has become a cause of violent behavior.
- We are aware of the breakdown of family structures, societal structures and value systems. We note these breakdowns are often accompanied by a distancing from the wellsprings of the wisdom of our religious traditions.
- We are aware of problematic images of religions in the media and the public eye. We note that often the worst of our religious traditions, in particular the most violent, is featured as representative of our religious traditions in their entirety.
- We are aware of the assault of the marketplace and its globalizing tendencies on our values and lifestyles, leading to a loss of vision, purpose and value in life. We note that many of the problematic forms that our religions have taken, particularly those associated

with religious extremism, are related to the power dynamics engendered by these globalizing tendencies.
- We are aware of a variety of crises that affect our own religious traditions, which we refer to as "The Crisis of the Holy." We note that none of our traditions is exempt from crisis, and that our crises are interrelated, tying the fates of all religions to global wellbeing.

The Response—A Turning to Wisdom

- We wish to express our recognition that there are no facile solutions to the ills of the world. At the same time, teachers of the wisdom of religious traditions, must do all they can to alleviate present suffering and to contribute to a solution of those problems that we can address.
- We wish to state our recognition that in the world's present state, all traditions have become interdependent, and must therefore face the challenges of the world in a collaborative manner.
- We wish to affirm our belief that within our traditions are resources of wisdom that can speak to the ills of society and the ills of religion.
- We wish to call upon all our religions to offer their finest teachings as resources to guide humanity to safe harbor, and to identify the teachings they can jointly offer a suffering humanity.
- We wish to further call upon practitioners of all religions to become aware of the life wisdom and spiritual wisdom of all religious traditions, as a means of obtaining a truer understanding of other religions, in the service of peaceful living.
- We invite thinkers and religious leaders to explore the possibility of addressing their own internal crises in light of the experiences and accumulated wisdom of other religious traditions.

Taking Care—Sharing Wisdom Responsibly

While we recognize the need of the hour points to opening towards the other, rather than to isolation, leading to violence and enmity, we call attention to the following considerations that are the basis of respectful learning and sharing between people, as individuals and as representatives of religious traditions

- Sharing Wisdom should never lead to the violation of the integrity of religious identity. Sharing Wisdom is not a means of influencing others to change or abandon their religious identity, but rather an invitation to deepen it and become more faithful to it.
- Sharing Wisdom should be done in a way that is mindful of power relations and considerations stemming from differences in wealth

distribution. It should not become a form of manipulation or coercion, whether personal or cultural.
- Sharing Wisdom has a broad universal mandate, almost a human right, grounded in the dignity of the human being, as understood diversely by our religious traditions. It is closely related to the right of religious freedom. As a spiritual process, it should be broadly open, beyond considerations of gender, caste and other forms of limitation.
- Sharing Wisdom should respect the integrity of religious teachings. It should not lead to the cheapening of teaching, nor to the loss of authenticity. Consequently, care must be taken to be mindful and respectful of broader theological structures, within which wisdom is couched, and to the internal processes, commitments and conditions that are necessary for successful realization of the age old wisdom of religious traditions.
- Sharing Wisdom should be accompanied by careful consideration of what forms of wisdom are most suitable to broad sharing with others and what forms require greater care and protection, in an effort to preserve their value and integrity.

Our Hope

It is our faith that the ills of the world and the ills of our religions may be addressed through an attitude of openness to sharing and learning from one another. In an increasingly interdependent world we are called to share our wisdom, to offer it to others, and to listen to what they in turn have to offer. It is our sincere hope and prayer that such sharing, carried out in the right spirit, will make our traditions better vehicles to achieve their designated purpose and will make the world a better and more peaceful place in which our religions and humanity can flourish.

NOTES

1. Indeed, some of the chapters in the present project indicate how in the process of sharing wisdom one is also opened up to self-criticism. See Volf, 12; Gianotti, 70 and elsewhere.
2. For an example of transformed self-understanding, see Sallie King's reference to Masao Abe's changed self-understanding in light of his dialogue with Christianity (60n5).
3. One example, in the case of Judaism, is how the message of non-violence made its way from Jainism, through the teachngs of Gandhi, into various attempts to locate this teaching within the fundamentally martial tradition of Judaism. Both the Buddhist and Hindu papers consider greater social awareness and enagement to be fruits of their tradition's exchange with other traditions. See Rambachan, 27; King, 47ff.
4. Ahluwalia, 35.
5. Volf, 5.
6. King, 56.

7. 28. It is worth noting that the call for common action that emerges from Meir Sendor's discussion, 88, based upon the teachings of R. Soloveitchik, sidesteps the wisdom of traditions, and focuses on common action as the sole area of mutual engagement. If "Sharing Wisdom" is taken seriously, one might suggest there is a qualitative difference between such collaboration and the effects of sharing wisdom as these are expressed in action, as in the cases of Hinduism and Buddhism, just quoted. Common action that is not inspired by wisdom is not tranformative in the same way. It may address a social ill, but it does not, in the process, transform religious understanding in a meaningful way. True sharing of wisdom would seem to always be transformative.

8. Rambachan, 25–26. See also Ahluwalia, 37. Sikhi's religious pluralism is thus of a piece with its understanding of divine wisdom. This is the same understanding articulated in Rambachan's presentation of Hinduism.

9. Members of the Elijah Board of World Religious Leaders who participated in the Amritsar meeting issued a statement of their own. This statement picks up on some of the ideas that the think tank had proposed in its own common vision. See http://elijah-interfaith.org/amritsar-statement.

ONE
A Christian Perspective

Miroslav Volf

We live in an age of great conflicts and petty hopes.

Take first our hopes. In the book *The Real American Dream*, Andrew Delbanco traced the history of the scope of American dreams—from the "holy God" of the Puritan founders, to the "great nation" of the nineteenth-century patriots, to the "satisfied self" of many today.[1] With some modifications, America may be in this regard indicative of trends in most societies that are highly integrated into the global market system. The idea of flourishing as a human being has shriveled to meaning no more than leading an experientially satisfying life. The sources of satisfaction may vary: power, possessions, love, religion, sex, food, drugs—whatever. What matters the most is not the *source* of satisfaction but the *experience* of it—*my* satisfaction. Our satisfied self is our best hope, and it is not petty. But a dark shadow of disappointment stubbornly follows this obsession with personal satisfaction. We are meant to live for something larger than our own satisfied selves. Petty hopes generate self-subverting, melancholy experiences.

Second, our world is caught in great conflicts (as well as in many small, even petty ones). Mostly these conflicts are fought along religious lines.[2] Christians and Muslims are clashing; so are Muslims and Jews, Hindus and Christians, Buddhists and Muslims, and so on. Though for the most part religions per se are not the causes of these conflicts, often religions legitimize and fuel them by enveloping mundane causes—often our petty hopes—with an aura of the sacred.

Most religions see as one of their main goals the opening up of self-absorbed individuals to connect them with a broader community and, indeed, with the source and goal of all reality. Similarly, most religions claim to contain important, even indispensable resources for fostering a culture of peace. But these two functions of religions are sometimes at odds with one another. When religions connect people with the divine, bring people together, and offer them a hope larger than mere self-fulfillment, communities with differing religious beliefs sometimes clash. When religions try to avoid legitimizing and fueling clashes between people, they often retreat into some private sphere and at times even reinforce people's self-absorption.

A central challenge for all religions in a pluralistic world is to *help people grow out of their petty hopes so as to live meaningful lives, and help them resolve their grand conflicts and live in communion with others*. That's where the importance of learning to share religious wisdom well comes in. If we as religious people fail to share wisdom well, we will fail both our many contemporaries who strive to live satisfied lives and yet remain deeply dissatisfied, and we will fail those who draw on their religious traditions to give meaning to their lives and yet remain mired in intractable and often deadly conflicts.

But how do we share religious wisdom well? I will address this question from a Christian perspective. Though there is no religiously generic way to share wisdom well (mainly because there is no generic religion), I hope that adherents of other religions will resonate with what I say, that they will find that it overlaps with how they believe the wisdom of their own tradition should be shared. But first let me say something about what, from that same perspective, wisdom is—and why share it.[3]

WHAT IS WISDOM?

Christians have traditionally understood their faith as an integrated way of life.[4] Correspondingly, Christian wisdom in one sense is that faith itself—an overarching interpretation of reality, a set of convictions, attitudes, and practices that direct people in living their lives well. Here "living well" means living as God created human beings to live, rather than living against the grain of their own true reality as well as the reality of the world. Wisdom in this sense is an integrated *way of life* that enables the flourishing of persons, communities, and all creation. Human beings are wise if they walk in that way.

Christians have also understood wisdom as something far more particular than a whole way of life, namely, as concrete *pieces of advice* about to *how* to flourish. When we read in the Proverbs, "A fool takes no pleasure in understanding but only in expressing personal opinion" (18:2), when Jesus says, "Give and it will be given to you" (Luke 6:38), when the Apostle Paul says, "Do not worry about anything" (Philippians 4:6), or when we read in the letter to the Ephesians, "Be kind to one another, tenderhearted, forgiving one another, as God in Christ has forgiven you"

(Ephesians 4:32), we are presented with wise advice, with what one may call "nuggets" of wisdom. Properly understood, these nuggets are components of wisdom as a way of life. Human beings are wise in this sense if they follow wise advice.

There is yet a third and most basic way in which Christians understand wisdom—surprisingly, perhaps, wisdom as a *person*.[5]

This immensely influential New Testament text contains echoes of both Jewish wisdom tradition (Proverbs) and Greek philosophical tradition (Logos). In the book of Proverbs wisdom is personified. She is the very beginning of God's creation, and she calls out to humans to listen to her and to flourish by obeying her (Proverbs 8). Christians have taken this "Lady Wisdom" to be the Word incarnate, Jesus Christ (John 1:1–14). The Apostle Paul also writes that Jesus Christ "has become for us wisdom from God" (1 Corinthians 1:30). Here human beings are wise if they follow Christ and, even more fundamentally, if they allow that personified Wisdom dwell in them, conform them to itself, and act through them (Gal. 2:20).

In all three senses just described, wisdom in the Christian sense is not a matter of personal taste or preference ("This strikes me as wise—for the time being!"), as "wisdom" often is for many people in dynamic, late-industrial societies. Neither is wisdom a marker of a group identity, a kind of beneficent custom ("This is wisdom for us, though not necessarily for you"), as it might be for some more "ethnic" religions or cultures. For Christians, wisdom is truth that concerns all people—and concerns them in the deepest way. To reject wisdom as a way of life, or Christ as the embodiment of wisdom, is not like leaving the dessert untouched after a good meal; rather, it is like refusing the very nourishment without which human beings cannot truly flourish.

This Christian claim is controversial, of course. Though it is not a negative statement about any religion or worldview, it is a claim that the Christian faith has the key to human beings succeeding not in this or that endeavor but in being human. But the aspect of it that a Muslim, for instance, might call into question is not the assertion that the wisdom of a particular religion is deemed indispensable, but that this claim applies to the Christian faith rather than to Islam. Controversial though it is, the claim is for most Christians necessary. Jewish monotheism introduced the idea of truth into the world of Western religions.[6] Christianity inherited that idea and radicalized it: The wisdom of faith is inextricably bound to the universal truth of faith.

For the sake of conciseness, when I explore on the following pages why and how to share wisdom I will usually simply lump these three senses of "wisdom" together. The disadvantage of doing so is obvious: when it comes to why and how to share wisdom, the differences among these three senses of wisdom matter a great deal. The reasons and manner of sharing wisdom understood as nuggets of advice, as a way of life, and as a Person only partly overlap. So I will point occasionally to differences in sharing wisdom in these three distinct senses, but I will have to leave it to my audience to fill in many blanks.

WHY SHARE WISDOM?

Before I get to specifically Christian reasons for sharing wisdom, let me suggest in general terms two conditions under which sharing wisdom makes sense.

Conditions for Sharing Wisdom

First, as a *single humanity* we live in *one world* Though there have always *been* only one humanity and one world, the processes of globalization, which have intensified during the last fifty years or so, have "shrunk" the world and made it possible concretely to *experience* (at least indirectly) humanity and the world as one. In this "shrunken" world we share religious wisdom just as we exchange millions of other things, from consumer goods to infectious diseases. One might even say that this planet-wide sharing of wisdom is part of the human condition in today's world.

Second, our single humanity is nevertheless internally *differentiated* — it is made up of diverse people belonging to diverse cultures and embracing diverse religions. It makes sense to share wisdom across religious boundaries because we are culturally and religiously different. If "the light" of all major religions were the very same light, with only the lamps from which it shines being different, then sharing religious wisdom across religious divides would make sense only weakly; it would serve as a reminder of what all religious people already know but have somehow forgotten. And yet, though diversity is an important condition for sharing wisdom, that diversity cannot be complete difference, total "otherness." If we were radically different from each other — if some of us were truly from Mars and others from Venus — we wouldn't know what to do with each other's wisdom when it was offered, or shared. We may not even recognize it *as* wisdom.

We can put the importance of both difference and sameness this way: If we were radically different, we wouldn't have "hands" to receive the wisdom shared by others; conversely, if we were completely alike we wouldn't have anything valuable to share. It is because we are both alike *and* different that it makes sense to share wisdom across religious dividing lines.

Reasons for Sharing Wisdom

Under these general conditions for sharing wisdom—humans being sharers, and their religions being sufficiently different so that each can benefit from sharing—Christians have specifically religious reasons for doing so.

First, they have an *obligation* to share wisdom. After his death and resurrection Jesus Christ said to his disciples: "As the Father has sent me, so I send you" (John 20:21)—with a mission to announce the Good News, and more broadly to share God's wisdom with the world. Christians share wisdom because Jesus Christ commanded them to do so.[7]

Second, the obligation to share wisdom is an expression of *love* for neighbors. Just as the Father's sending of Jesus was rooted in God's love for the world (John 3:16), so also is the Christian's mission rooted in love for fellow human beings. Christians share wisdom to help needy people find meaning in life, resolve conflicts in which they are deeply mired, get motivated to feed the hungry and clothe the naked, and in general because they desire to prevent others from languishing or even perishing as a result of living "out of sync" with the way in which God created them to live.[8]

Ultimately, however, Christians don't share wisdom merely out of obedience to a command, and not even simply out of love for neighbors. In reality they share it—or at least should share it—primarily because the Wisdom dwelling in them *seeks to impart itself* through them to others. As the Apostle Paul puts it, the "love of Christ" urges [them] on (2 Cor. 5:14).

These religious motivations to share wisdom *fit the character of the Christian faith* as religion. Put rather generally, along with some other major world religions Christianity is a monotheistic faith of a prophetic type. Take first the significance of *monotheism* for sharing wisdom. When it comes to God's relation to the world, there is a strict correlation between the divine "One" and the mundane "whole." Since God is One, God is the God of reality as a whole. The wisdom of the one God is the wisdom for the whole of humanity, not just a segment of it. It should, therefore, be shared with all.

The thrust toward sharing generated by monotheism is reinforced by the prophetic character of the Christian faith. Religions of the prophetic type are structured by two basic movements: ascent to the realm of the divine (encounter with God, deep study of scriptures, and the like), and return with a message for the world—a twofold movement illustrated well by the account in the Gospels according to which Jesus began his public ministry by fasting in the wilderness (or, to use an example from another major prophetic religion, by the story about how, after ascending to the highest heavens into the very presence of God, the Prophet Muhammad returned to continue his world-transforming mission). In the ascent, religious persons acquire wisdom and are transformed; in the return, they share wisdom with fellow human beings in order to transform the world. The ascent doesn't happen simply so that the believer will benefit from the encounter with God (as in mystical religions); it happens for the purpose of the return, so that the world will be mended and brought into greater conformity with God's designs for it.

ON REFRAINING FROM SHARING WISDOM

Christians have powerful reasons to share religious wisdom with others. And on the whole, throughout history they haven't shied from doing so (though in some periods their cross-cultural missionary impulse has been subdued, as in the case of Protestants from their inception in 1517 to about 1794, when William Carey started the modern Protestant missionary movement).[9] There are situations, however, in which it may be unwise to share religious wisdom. In the Sermon on the Mount, Jesus Christ famously and harshly warned: "Do not give what is holy to dogs; and do not throw your pearls before swine, or they will trample them under foot and turn and maul you" (Matthew 7:6). These severe words are a reminder that relations between religions are sometimes very tense, even violent. In such circumstances—for example, of religious persecution, which has been historically and geographically widespread and in certain places continues unabated today[10]—attempts at sharing wisdom may elicit both angry incomprehension and further violence. Sometimes wisdom counsels not to be shared. At other times, notwithstanding the severity of opposition, courageous wisdom will cry out to be heard just so as to expose the foolishness of the opponents.

HOW SHOULD ONE SHARE WISDOM?

When done well, sharing wisdom can be likened to the giving and receiving of gifts. Before we go into the specifics of how to give and receive wisdom and how not to do so, note one important feature of sharing wisdom: It is more like playing a musical piece for a friend than treating her to a meal. When I give food to a friend, what she eats I no longer have; in contrast, when I play music for her, she receives something that I continue to possess. When I share wisdom, I don't part with what I give; to the contrary, I may come to "possess" it in an even deeper way.[11]

What does it mean to share wisdom well? How does one share it responsibly? I will explore these questions by examining how we should act both as givers and receivers of wisdom.

The Self as Giver

From the very inception of the church, Christians witnessed publicly about their faith. The church was born on the day of Pentecost,[12] and on that occasion the disciples of the crucified and resurrected Jesus Christ spoke about him in many languages to people from many parts of the world. They actively shared the wisdom of their faith—its nuggets, its whole way of life, and the Wisdom incarnate.

For Christians, giving *witness* is a key way of sharing wisdom. But what does it mean to witness well? First, a witness is *not a tyrant* who imposes. True, throughout a long history Christians have sometimes sought to impose their faith by the sword,[13] by the power of rhetorical manipulation, or with inducements of material gain. Yet imposition stands starkly at odds with the basic character of the Christian faith, which is at its heart about self-giving—God's self-giving and human self-giving—and not about self-imposing. Karl Barth, a great Protestant theologian of the past century, put it correctly: In relation to non-Christians (and to fellow Christians!), followers of Christ are in the position of John the Baptist as depicted in the famous painting of Matthias Grunewald, namely, at the foot of the cross with an outstretched hand simply pointing to the crucified Christ.[14] Far from imposing the wisdom of faith, they don't even offer it as something they themselves give—properly, they merely to point to the Wisdom. That Wisdom offers itself; some will partake, and others refuse.[15]

Second, a witness is not a *merchant* who sells. Deeply enmeshed as we moderns are in economic exchanges, we live in cultures pervaded by the activity of buying and selling.[16] Often we treat religions and their wisdom as commodities to be bought and sold. Although there are good reasons to remunerate priests, pastors, and other religious leaders, neither they nor unpaid lay people are not sellers of wisdom—certainly they are no more sellers of wisdom than good teachers are of knowledge or good doctors of cures.[17] Wisdom is betrayed when it is sold and bought. Sellers are tempted to seduce buyers into making a purchase by tailoring the merchandise to fit the desires of buyer; the act of selling often distorts wisdom and leaves buyers with a festering suspicion that the seller has taken advantage of them. Buyers, on the other hand, pick and choose, and purchase as much or as little as they see fit. When bought and sold, wisdom doesn't shape people's lives but at best merely satisfies already existing desires—none of which the wisdom itself has crafted, and to all of which wisdom is subservient. Treated as a commodity, wisdom deteriorates into a technique of helping people live the way they please, even when the way they please to live is thoroughly unwise.[18]

In the Christian tradition at its best, wisdom is given freely. The prophet Isaiah writes, "Ho, everyone who thirsts come to the waters; and you that have no money, come, buy and eat! Come, buy wine and milk without money and without price" (Isaiah 55:1). Jesus echoed these words when he said, "Come to me, all you that are weary and carrying heavy burdens, and I will give you rest" (Matthew 11:28). Christian wisdom is fundamentally about what God gives free of charge and must therefore be imparted free of charge.[19] A good witness will resist the commodification of wisdom.

Third, as witnesses Christians are not mere *teachers* who instruct. A teacher can learn something that remains very much external to her own life and then pass it on as useful information to others (say in the way a math professor may teach trigonometry). Christians, in contrast, should witness as those who not only speak about Christ with their words but also imitate him in their behavior and entrust themselves to his care in their living and dying. When they witness, then, they are offering a way of life in which they themselves participate. Consequently, the more "indwelled" by Wisdom they are, the better sharers of wisdom they will be.

Fourth, a witness is not a mere *midwife*. The great Greek teacher of wisdom Socrates saw himself in the role of a midwife. His task was to help birth the wisdom with which every person was already pregnant. Not unlike Buddha in his view of enlightenment, Socrates saw himself as incidental to the process of acquiring wisdom.[20] According to this view, if a person is sufficiently self-aware, she can find her own way to wisdom, for wisdom resides within her.

Not so with Christ, and not so with a witness to Christ. Christ does not help a person find the wisdom hidden in her own soul; Christ *is* the wisdom.[21] Consequently a follower of Christ is a witness to Christ, whose purpose is to direct the attention of a person away from herself to Christ, to the life, death, and resurrection of the Word incarnate, who lived in a specific time and place. Socrates helps a person discover something inside herself; in contrast, a witness to Christ tells a person about something that has occurred outside herself, something about which she must be informed.[22] So a witness points not only away from himself but also away from the person to whom he is giving witness; he points to Christ and the wisdom he was and continues to be.

The Other as Receiver

Good givers will respect the integrity of receivers. There are limits to what others may be willing or able to receive, and givers should honor these limits. Christians should share wisdom in the way that the first letter of St. Peter instructs them to give an account of their hope—"with gentleness and reverence" (1 Peter 3:15–16).

It is relatively easy to honor others' limits when it comes to sharing nuggets of wisdom. The receivers can integrate these bits of wise advice into their own overarching interpretations of life without much disruption. Often, though, what is received takes on a different flavor from what is given. Chicken in Thai food tastes different from the way it tastes in a mustard and mayonnaise sandwich. A nugget of wisdom in one "dish" of religion will taste different when served with a different set of ingredients. More prosaically put, receivers will often gratefully receive what is offered but tweak it to fit into their overarching interpretation of life.

Granting the right of others to receive what they want and do with it as they please is part of the respect that givers afford to recipients. There is some reason for concern, however, about sharing one's nuggets of wisdom in the fast-paced, media-saturated, salad-bar culture in which many of us live. First, givers themselves often dilute their wisdom to make it palatable to as many buyers as possible. Second, receivers often do not insert newly acquired nuggets of wisdom into an overarching interpretation of life. The nuggets remain free-floating bits of advice that are used when convenient and discarded when not. This selective employment of wisdom-out-of-context then contributes to making an unwise way of life more acceptable—certainly not the goal of sharing wisdom!

Sharing wisdom as a way of life becomes even more complicated. The most significant limits to what others are able to receive are set by their fear of losing their identity. For if they take too much from the "outside," their reception of wisdom may feel like an unwelcome undoing of their very selves. To receive Christ as Wisdom or to receive faith as an overarching interpretation of life may seem profoundly alienating to the would-be taker. But it goes without saying in a paper on sharing wisdom written from a Christian perspective that embracing a Christian way of life *can be*, and *mostly is*, experienced as a return to our own proper selves.

The Christian tradition has always accounted for the real possibility that others may see the highest wisdom to which it points as mere foolishness.[23] A way of life in which self-giving is praised and the exercise of power over others suspected appears to some as folly, not wisdom.[24] So also does the idea that Jesus Christ saves through his death on the cross.[25] Wisdom may not appear wise at first. For people to recognize it *as* wisdom, they must have some affinity with it—they must have eyes to see and ears to hear, as the prophet Ezekiel put it (Ezekiel 12:1–2).[26] That's why some important strands in the Christian tradition suggest that people can receive Wisdom only when God's Spirit creates in them the right conditions for its reception.[27]

Notice that in two crucial regards—at the point of giving and at the point of receiving—it is not Christians themselves who do the most important work in sharing wisdom. Ultimately they cannot give it; for Christ must give wisdom. And ultimately they cannot force others to receive wisdom; God's Spirit must open people's eyes to see it. When Christians are at their very best in sharing wisdom, they are channels through which God imparts wisdom. The book of Acts expresses this basic idea clearly when reporting the first conversions to the way of Christ: it wasn't the Apostles who converted people through their preaching—it was *God* who added people to the church (Acts 2:47).

The Self as Receiver

As we share the wisdom of our religious traditions, we should keep in mind that the person to whom we offer wisdom is also a giver, not just a passive receiver. As givers, we respect receivers by seeing ourselves as potential receivers, too. Yet many religious people have found it difficult to think of themselves as receiving anything of substance from other religions, for they are already embracing what they likely believe is a— even *the*—true and salutary way of life. That perspective is certainly true of many Christians. Doesn't John's Gospel say that Christ is "the way, the truth, and the life" (14:6)? Doesn't the Letter to the Colossians state that in Christ are "hidden all the treasures of wisdom and knowledge" (2:3)? How, then, can Christians receive any significant wisdom from others?

This question is suggesting that receiving wisdom from others might not be possible, when that has in fact indisputably taken place! It isn't at all difficult to demonstrate that Christians have received wisdom from others in the past and that they continue to do so. Two examples from the distant past will suffice. The first is Christianity's appropriation of the spiritual treasures of Judaism. With some minor modifications, for instance, the Christian Old Testament is the Hebrew Bible, made up of texts that by themselves comprised the sacred scriptures of the early Christians. Second, Christianity's early encounter with Greek language and culture meant its inevitably (though for the most part unintentionally) receiving of Greek wisdom.[28] A rich vocabulary of faith comes to the theology and everyday liturgical life of Christians from the Greek philosophical tradition (even if major philosophical terms have been partly transformed when appropriated).[29] Indeed, more broadly than in Christianity's encounter with ancient Greek culture, the Christian faith has received wisdom every time the gospel has been translated into another language and taken root in a different cultural environment.[30]

So how can Christians, who believe that all wisdom resides in and emanates from Jesus Christ, receive the wisdom of others? The answer, though not entirely obvious to all, is simple even if it is not easy to see all its implications clearly. Jesus Christ is the incarnate Word—Wisdom!— through whom "all things came into being" and who is "the light of all people," as one of the most influential texts of the New Testament, the Prologue to the Gospel of John, puts it (John 1:3–4). Echoing the text of John's Gospel, early church father Justin Martyr described the wisdom of Greek philosophers as "parts of the Word" and "seeds of truth."[31]

Accordingly, all light, wherever encountered, is the light of the Word and therefore Christ's light; all wisdom, whoever speaks it, is Christ's wisdom. It cannot be otherwise if *all things* come into being and exist through the Word who became incarnate in Christ. Granted, that's a big "if," one that non-Christians will be unwilling to accept. But at issue here are the stances of Christians, not their plausibility to non-Christians. Accept the condition ("all things came into being" through Christ), and the consequence ("all wisdom is Christ's wisdom") follows ineluctably.

But Christians already have Christ, one could object. Why accept anything from others, even if one grants that they possess "seeds" of Wisdom? First, there is a depth and breadth to Christ, the Wisdom, that remains always unplumbed by his followers. Put somewhat more abstractly, the object of faith—God, who dwells in inapproachable light—is never fully present in the consciousness and practice of the faithful, not just because they are creatures and God is the creator but because they are shaped by the particular situations in which they live. Second, along with others Christians live in a stream of time that throws at human beings ever-new challenges. Often they find themselves disoriented and uncertain as to how to bring the Wisdom of Christ to bear upon new situations. That's where the phenomenon that another twentieth-century Protestant theologian, Paul Tillich, comes in, namely, the phenomenon called "reverse prophetism"[32]: Christians can receive from the outside a prophetic challenge to alter their convictions and practices so as to address more adequately the problems of the day with the resources of the Wisdom they embrace.[33]

As the relationship between "the Word" and "parts of the Word" suggests, any wisdom that Christians receive from others must resonate with the scriptural narratives about Christ as interpreted by the great teachers of the church. Compatibility with these narratives is for Christians the criterion that determines what is wisdom and what is not, what may come in and what must stay out. Of course, it is possible to give up on these narratives—indeed, one may come to believe that it would be foolish *not* to give up on them. But a person who comes to this conclusion has abandoned the Christian faith either in favor of another way of life (say Jainism or the philosophy of Nietzsche) or in favor of relating to all ways of life in the manner in which she approaches a salad-bar—picking and choosing what suits her, and disregarding the rest.

SHARING WISDOM—LOVE AND FORGIVENESS

One way to describe what I have suggested in the main body of this chapter is to say that the sharing of wisdom should be an enactment of neighborly love.

When we share wisdom, we give and receive, and giving and receiving should be an exercise in love. Jesus Christ, the Wisdom, is the embodiment of God's love for humanity, and he summed up both "the law and the prophets" and the "love command" when he issued the Golden Rule: "In everything do to others as you would have them do to you" (Matthew 7:12). "Everything" encompasses the sharing of wisdom. For neighborly love to define how wisdom should be shared means that the act of sharing wisdom should harmonize with the content of what is shared.[34]

As mentioned earlier, however, over the centuries Christians have sometimes shared wisdom in ways diametrically opposed to the requirements of the very wisdom they have inherited—manipulatively, forcibly, even murderously.[35] Similarly, Christians themselves have suffered greatly from the imposition of others' wisdom on them. Claims that more Christians were persecuted and killed on account of their faith in the past one hundred years than in the entire priory history of the church may be exaggerated,[36] but persecutions of Christian under Lenin and Stalin in the Soviet Union and Mao in China were brutal and massive by all accounts.[37]

When human beings are wronged, as in such relations between Christians and non-Christians, forgiveness and repentance are called for. That's what Christian wisdom teaches. The injunction to forgive may seem like just one "nugget" of Christian wisdom. It is that, but also much more. It is the defining stance of Jesus Christ, the Wisdom personified, and a central pillar of the Christian way of life.[38] Let me briefly note some key elements of forgiveness and relate them to wronging that happens when Christians and adherents of other religions share wisdom poorly. Forgiveness itself is like a gift. And just as a gift must be received in order truly to be given, so also does forgiveness. We receive forgiveness by repenting—by naming our objectionable deeds as wrongs, by grieving over the injury inflicted, and by determining to mend our ways. It is crucial for Christians to examine honestly the way they have shared their wisdom in the past, see themselves in the proper light—purify their memory, as the late Saint Pope John Paul II put it[39]—and, where appropriate, admit to wrongs and correct their ways. Of course, non-Christians would do well to do the same. Still, in cases of mutual wronging, Christian conviction dictates that one's repentance does not depend on that of the other party, if we have wronged each other, I need to repent regardless of whether you repent.

More radically, Christian wisdom teaches that forgiveness doesn't even depend on the repentance of the wrongdoer—a notion that may press the limits of what from the Christian tradition is shareable with other traditions. Human beings were reconciled to God in Christ apart from their repentance. "Christ died for the ungodly"—*all* ungodly— writes the Apostle Paul with stunning radicalness. (Romans 5:6). So also, the followers of Christ must forgive apart from wrongdoers' repentance. The gift of forgiveness should be given not as a reward for repentance but in the hope that the gift itself will help the wrongdoer receive it by repenting. Forgiving and sharing wisdom are similar in this one important regard: they are forms of gift giving. One acts first by giving a gift—and then waits to see whether or not the other will freely receive it.

Why forgiveness first, and then repentance? Because the goal of forgiveness is not simply to lighten the forgiver's psychological burden, not even simply to diffuse conflict, but above all to return the offender to the good and, ultimately, to restore communion between the wrongdoer and the wronged. Those who follow Christ, writes Martin Luther,

> Grieve more over the sin of their offenders than over the loss or offense to themselves. And they do this that they may recall those offenders from their sin rather than avenge the wrongs they themselves have suffered. Therefore, they put off the form of their own righteousness and put on the form of those others, praying for their persecutors, blessing those who curse, doing good to the evil-doers, preparing to pay the penalty and make satisfaction for their very enemies that they may be saved. This is the Gospel and the example of Christ.[40]

When Christians are wronged in the process of sharing wisdom—or more broadly, in any encounters with other people—they ought to forgive. To forgive is to do two things at once. First, it is to name a suffered wrong *as* wrong. To forgive isn't to deny or even overlook the wrongdoing, rather, to condemn it. No forgiveness without condemnation. But if condemnation is a necessary presupposition of forgiveness, the heart of forgiveness is something else. For to forgive is, second, not to let the wrongdoing count against the wrongdoer. He deserves punishment, but he gets the opposite. He gets grace.

Since forgiveness lies at the heart of Christian wisdom, as the above quotation from Martin Luther aptly expresses, for Christians to refuse to forgive is not just to fail to repair a short circuit in the sharing of wisdom—it is to contradict wisdom itself. To forgive *is* to share wisdom— perhaps even among the most efficacious ways of doing so.

SHARING WISDOM: GRAND CONFLICTS, PETTY HOPES

In conclusion, let me return to grand conflicts and petty hopes. How should we share wisdom so as not to reinforce religious conflicts but instead help sustain and promote peace? We need to resist the temptation to "help" wisdom gain a footing in people's lives by manipulating or forcing others to embrace wisdom. Similarly, we need to resist the lure of pridefully perceiving ourselves as only givers of wisdom, rather than always also its receivers—and receivers from both expected and unexpected sources. If we give in to these tendencies, we will add to religious conflicts rather than preparing the soil in which religious faith can help resolve them. From a Christian perspective, all our efforts at sharing wisdom should focus on allowing wisdom to shape our own lives and show itself in all its attractiveness, reasonableness, and usefulness. We need to trust that it will make itself embraceable by others if it is going to be embraced at all. In that way, as sharers of wisdom we honor both the power of wisdom and the integrity of its potential recipients.

How should we share wisdom so as not to feed petty hopes but instead help persons connect meaningfully with communities—small and large—and with the source and goal of the universe? We need to resist the temptation to "package" religious wisdom in attractive and digestible "nuggets" that a person can take up and insert into some doomed project of striving to live a merely experientially satisfying life. If we were to do so, wisdom would serve folly. From a Christian perspective, sharing religious wisdom makes sense only if that wisdom is allowed to counter the multiple manifestations of self-absorption by givers and receivers and to connect them with what ultimately matters—God, whom we should love with all our being, and neighbors, whom we should love as ourselves.

NOTES

1. Andrew Delbanco, *The Real American Dream. A Meditation on Hope* (Cambridge, MA: Harvard University Press, 1999).

2. See Jonathan Fox, "Religion and State Failure," *International Political Science Review* 25 (2004): 55–76; Jonathan Fox, "The Rise of Religious Nationalism and Conflict," *Journal of Peace Research* 41 (2004): 715–31; David Herbert and John Wolffe, "Religion and Contemporary Conflict in Historical Perspective," in *Religion in History: Conflict, Conversion, and Coexistence*, ed. John Wolffe (Manchester, UK: Manchester University Press, 2004), 286–320.

3. For a compelling book on Christian wisdom, see David F. Ford, *Christian Wisdom: Desiring God and Learning in Love* (Cambridge: Cambridge University Press, 2007).

4. On Christian faith as a way of life, see Miroslav Volf, *Against the Tide: Love in a Time of Petty Dreams and Persisting Enmities* (Grand Rapids, MI: Eerdmans, 2010), 82–85. See also Christian Scharen, *Faith as a Way of Life* (Grand Rapids, MI: Eerdmans, 2008). Many Muslims see Islam as a way of life. Obviously, Christians and Muslims mean rather different things by a way of life, and within each religion, extremists, such as Sayyid Qutb, whose account of Islam as a way of life I discuss in the introduction, mean partly different things than those faithful to the classical tradition in each religion. And yet most Muslims and Christians agree: their "religion" is not merely a set of convictions or a set of rituals but a way of living in the world today. Interestingly enough, the phrase "way of life," emptied of its deeper meaning, comes up even in the rhetoric of Western politicians in their legitimate opposition to radical Islam. They see it as a threat to "our way of life" (see President George W. Bush's address to a joint session of Congress from September 20, 2001, available at http://www.washingtonpost.com/wp-srv/nation/specials/attacked/transcripts/bushaddress_092001.html).

5. "In the beginning was the Word, and the Word was with God, and the Word was God. He was with God in the beginning. Through him all things were made; without him nothing was made that has been made. In him was life, and that life was

the light of men. The light shines in the darkness, but the darkness has not understood it. There was a man sent from God, whose name was John" (John 1:1–6).

This immensely influential New Testament text contains echoes of both Jewish wisdom tradition (Proverbs) and Greek philosophical tradition (Logos).

6. See Jan Assmann, *Die Mosaische Unterscheidung: Oder der Preis des Monotheismus* (Munich: Carl Hanser, 2003); and Jan Assmann, *Moses the Egyptian* (Cambridge, MA: Harvard University Press, 1998).

7. On the "great commission," see David J. Bosch, "The Structure of Mission," in *Exploring Church Growth*, ed. Wilbert R. Shenk (Grand Rapids, MI: Eerdmans, 1983), 218–48; Peter T. O'Brien, "The Great Commission of Matthew 28:18–20," *Reformed Theological Review* 35 (1976): 66–78; Tom Wright, *Matthew for Everyone: Part Two* (Louisville: Westminster John Knox, 2004), 204–6.

8. On the "great commandment" as motivation for sharing, see Augustine, *On Christian Doctrine* 1.26, 27–29, 30; Augustine, *Letter 130*, 14.

9. See William Carey, *An Enquiry into the Obligations of Christians to Use Means for the Conversion of the Heathens* (Leicester: Ann Ireland, 1792).

10. See Catherine Cookson, ed., *The Encyclopedia of Religious Freedom* (London: Routledge, 2003). The U.S. Commission on International Religious Freedom publishes an annual report assessing the global state of religious freedom and persecution. See http://www.uscirf.gov.

11. On noncompetitive forms of giving, see Kathryn Tanner, *Jesus, Humanity, and the Trinity: A Brief Systematic Theology* (Minneapolis, MN: Fortress, 2001), 90–94.

12. On the day of Pentecost as the birth of the church, see Jürgen Moltmann, *The Church in the Power of the Spirit: A Contribution to Messianic Ecclesiology* (Minneapolis, MN: Fortress, 1993).

13. The most egregious example is the conquest of the Americas. See Bartolomé de las Casas, *The Devastation of the Indies: A Brief Account*, trans. Herma Briffault (Baltimore: Johns Hopkins University Press, 1992); George E. Tinker, *Missionary Conquest: The Gospel and Native American Cultural Genocide* (Minneapolis, MN: Augsburg Fortress, 1993); Josep M. Barnadas, "The Catholic Church in Colonial Spanish America," and Eduardo Hoonaert, "The Catholic Church in Colonial Brazil," in *Colonial Latin America*, vol. 1, *The Cambridge History of Latin America*, ed. Leslie Bethell (Cambridge: Cambridge University Press, 1984), 511–40, 541–56. See also the now classic work, Tzvetan Todorov's *The Conquest of America: The Question of the Other* (New York, Harper & Row, 1984).

14. See Barth, *Church Dogmatics* IV/3.2, 797.

15. This is an expression of the fact that, strictly speaking, Christians do not possess wisdom. Christ being wisdom incarnate, it is the other way around. Properly understood, Christians are possessed by wisdom, and are wise not in themselves but just to the degree that wisdom dwells in them.

16. On the increasing commodification of everyday exchanges, see the essays in Susan Strasser, ed., *Commodifying Everything: Relationships of the Market* (London: Routledge, 2003).

17. On the importance of gift giving in human life, see Volf, *Free of Charge*, 55–126.

18. Though the apostle Paul thought that he had the right to be paid for his apostolic work, he forwent remuneration (see Acts 20:33–35; 1 Cor. 9:1–18; 2 Thess. 3:8). Socrates, as is well known, would not receive remuneration for his services (see Plato, *Apology*, 19d–e).

19. See Volf, *Free of Charge*.

20. See Plato, *Theaetetus* 148e–50e.

21. See Søren Kierkegaard, *Philosophical Fragments*, trans. David F. Swenson and Howard V. Hong (Princeton, NJ: Princeton University Press, 1962), 11–45.

22. On "hearing" as fundamental to faith, see Joseph Cardinal Ratzinger (Benedict XVI), *Introduction to Christianity* (San Francisco: Ignatius Press, 1990), 90–92.

23. "Jews demand miraculous signs and Greeks look for wisdom, but we preach Christ crucified: a stumbling block to Jews and foolishness to Gentiles, but to those

whom God has called, both Jews and Greeks, Christ the power of God and the wisdom of God. For the foolishness of God is wiser than man's wisdom, and the weakness of God is stronger than man's strength" (1 Corinthians 1:22–25).

24. For a literary exploration of this theme, see Paer Lagerkvist, *Barabbas*, trans. Alan Blair (New York: Vintage, 1989).

25. Sayyid Qutb, for instance, explicitly states that, while living in the West, he engaged in polemics with Christians, trying to show them the unreasonableness of Christianity: "Look at these concepts of the Trinity, Original Sin, Sacrifice, and Redemption, which are agreeable neither to reason nor to conscience" (Qutb, *Milestones*, 95).

26. On the ability of disciples to perceive Christ, see a critical comment by Friedrich Nietzsche that presupposes the same conviction about the need for affinity between what is encountered and what is received (Nietzsche, *Twilight of the Idols and The Anti-Christ*,157). See also Volf, *Exclusion and Embrace*, 254–58.

27. So, for instance, Kierkegaard, *Philosophical Fragments*, 14–15.

28. See on this Werner W. Jaeger, *Early Christianity and Greek Paideia* (Cambridge, MA: Harvard University Press, 1961); and Jaroslav Pelikan, *Christianity and Classical Culture: The Metamorphosis of Natural Theology in the Christian Encounter with Hellenism* (New Haven, CT: Yale University Press, 1993).

29. On the transformation of the adopted Greek philosophical vocabulary to suit the needs of the subject matter as understood by the Christian faith, see, among many others, John D. Zizioulas, "The Doctrine of the Holy Trinity: The Significance of the Cappadocian Contribution," in *Trinitarian Theology Today: Essays on Divine Being and Act*, ed. Christoph Schwöbel (Edinburgh: T&T Clark, 1995), 44–60.

30. On the phenomenon of give and take in the process of inculturation, see Chibueze Udeani, *Inculturation as Dialogue: Igbo Culture and the Message of Christ* (New York, Rodopi, 2007), 130–33.

31. "There seem to be seeds of truth among all men" (First Apology, 44).

"We have been taught that Christ is the first-born of God, and we have declared above that He is the Word of whom every race of men were partakers; and those who lived reasonably are Christians, even though they have been thought atheists" (First Apology, 46).

"For whatever either lawgivers or philosophers uttered well, they elaborated by finding and contemplating some part of the Word. But since they did not know the whole of the Word, which is Christ, they often contradicted themselves" (Second Apology, 10).

The texts from Justin Martyr (100–165 AD) come from his apologetic writings. He strives to show not only the reasonableness but also the superiority of the Christian faith. In the process, he addresses in a way that has proven seminal for a good deal of Christian history the issue of how it is that there is significant truth in other religions and philosophies so that Christians can indeed learn something from them. His solution to the problem is to claim that Christ is the Word but that non-Christians possess the "seeds of truth" and "parts" of the Word. This approach presupposes that the Word, which is incarnate in Jesus Christ, can make itself known even where the Christian faith is not embraced or even proclaimed.

32. Paul Tillich, *Systematic Theology*, vol. 3 (Chicago: University of Chicago Press, 1963), 214.

33. With regard to Christians learning from Muslims, in *Allah* I write the following: "Each faith has a repertoire of beliefs and practices. At a given time or place, a faith will foreground some themes in its repertoire and background others. Currently, for instance, 'submission to God,' Islam's central theme, is not a favorite 'melody' of many Christians in the West; it runs counter to Western egalitarian cultural sensibilities. But it's an essential and oft 'performed' part of the historic Christian repertoire. After all, Christians believe that God is the sovereign Lord. It would be fully legitimate, and maybe even desirable, for Christians in the West, partly nudged by Muslims, to rediscover 'submission to God' as a key dimension of spirituality" (197).

34. For a brief discussion of some basic rules for evangelism based on the Golden Rule, see ibid., chap. 11.

35. Martin E. Marty's book *The Christian World: A Global History* (New York: Random House, 2007), includes numerous examples of Christians sharing wisdom in both good and bad ways.

36. This claim became popular following the publication of the Italian journalist Antonio Socci's book *The New Persecuted*, only available in the original Italian: *I Nuovo Perseguitati* (Casale Monferrato: Piemme, 2002). Socci derives many of his figures from David B. Barrett, George T. Kurian, and Todd M. Johnson, *The World Christian Encyclopedia*, 2 vols. (Oxford: Oxford University Press, 2001), which has been the subject of several criticisms. For an impartial assessment of the encyclopedia's data, see Becky Hsu et al., "Estimating the Religious Composition of All Nations: An Empirical Assessment of the World Christian Database," *Journal for the Scientific Study of Religion* 47 (2008): 678–93.

37. See Robert Conquest, "The Churches and the People," in *The Harvest of Sorrow: Soviet Collectivization and the Terror-famine* (Oxford: Oxford University Press, 1986), 199–213; Geoffrey A. Hosking, "Religion and Nationality under the Soviet State," in *The First Socialist Society: A History of the Soviet Union from Within*, rev. ed. (Cambridge, MA: Harvard University Press, 1993), 227–60; Richard C. Bush Jr., *Religion in Communist China* (Nashville: Abingdon, 1970); G. Thompson Brown, *Christianity in the People's Republic of China*, rev. ed. (Atlanta: John Knox, 1986), 75–134.

38. As noted in his fundamental instruction on prayer: "This, then, is how you should pray: 'Our Father in heaven, hallowed be your name, your kingdom come, your will be done on earth as it is in heaven. Give us today our daily bread. Forgive us our debts, as we also have forgiven our debtors. And lead us not into temptation, but deliver us from the evil one.' For if you forgive me when they sin against you, your heavenly Father will also forgive you. But if you do not forgive men their sins, your Father will not forgive your sins" (Matthew, 6:9–15). On forgiveness, see further Volf, *Free of Charge*, chapters 4–6.

39. See John Paul II, "Jubilee Characteristic: The Purification of Memory," *Origins* 29 (2000): 649–50.

40. Martin Luther, *Works*, vol. 31, ed. Harold J. Grimm (Philadelphia: Fortress, 1962), 306.

TWO
A Hindu Perspective

Anantanand Rambachan

WHAT IS WISDOM?

In the Rāmacaritamānasa, a sixteenth century Hindi vernacular poetic reworking of the story of Rama by Tulasidasa, Lakshmana, the brother of Rama, in the familiar Hindu style of a disciple questioning a teacher, respectfully asks a number of questions.[1] Among his many questions is a request for an explanation of the nature of wisdom (*jñāna*). Rama's characterization of the nature of wisdom wastes no words and goes to the heart of the Hindu teaching.

> Wisdom is freedom from self-centeredness; it is seeing God present equally in all.[2]

Rama's distillation of the meaning of wisdom reverberates throughout the Hindu tradition and is articulated similarly in various sacred texts. The Bhagavadgita (13:27), for example, identifies the discernment of the divine with true seeing or wisdom.[3]

> One who sees the Supreme God existing equally in all beings, the Imperishable in the perishable, truly sees.[4]

These texts, and countless others, make two significant wisdom disclosures, both of which are logical and consistent with the Hindu understanding of the nature of God.[5] The first is the disclosure that God is present in all beings. With respect to the presence of God, all beings must be equally regarded. No one can be excluded and no qualifications can be introduced. Wisdom does not limit the divine presence to the human species. Other life forms must also be within the reach of our concern and compassion. The second wisdom disclosure is the emphasis on the equality of divine presence. This presence does not admit of any variation. It rules out any argument that attempts to justify inequality and injustice on the basis of an unequal divine presence. Wisdom is the ability to see everything in a new light. The ordinary becomes extra-ordinary when seen as infused with divinity.

Although wisdom is identified in the Hindu tradition with "seeing" the inclusivity and equality of God, such seeing, it must be emphasized, is more than verbal knowledge. The Bhagavadgita (2:42), speaks critically of those who delight merely in the words of the sacred text (*vedavādaratāḥ*). The same text, in a series of verses (55–72), characterizes wisdom as an integrated mode of being. Wisdom is present when knowing and being coincides. Wisdom is identified with freedom from greed and with delight and contentment in God. It is equated with liberation from fear and anger. Most importantly, wisdom is the ability to identify with others in happiness and in suffering. The Bhagavadgita (6:32) praises this empathetic way of being as the culmination of Yoga and commends the wise person (5:25; 12:4) as one who rejoices in the well-being of all (*sarvabhūtahite ratāḥ*). The wise is "One who hates no one, who is friendly and compassionate, non-possessive and unselfish, balanced in suffering and pleasure and forgiving."

WHY SHARE WISDOM?

The often-cited Ṛg Veda (1.89.1) text, "Let noble truths come to us from all sides," expresses the deep and ancient Hindu value for sharing and receiving wisdom. At the conclusion of the Bhagavadgita (18:67–71) the teacher Krishna commends the sharing of his teachings. He characterizes the sharing of wisdom as the dearest form of service and the teacher as dearest to him among human beings (18: 69). This unmistakable value for wisdom in the Hindu tradition has to been seen in the context of the widely shared understanding of the fundamental human problem as one of ignorance (*avidyā*).

As already noted, wisdom is equated with the discernment of God in all and all in God. This is expressed in similes and metaphors. One of the most striking of these in the Bhagavadgita (7:7) likens God to the string in a necklace of jewels. "On Me," says Krishna, "all this universe is strung like pearls on a string." Elsewhere in the Bhagavadgita (9:6), all beings are described as abiding and moving in God: "As the mighty wind, going everywhere, dwells always in space, so all beings dwell in Me." The human problem therefore, in relation to God, is not one of overcoming a spatial or temporal separation between oneself and God. The impossibility of any form of separation from God leads to a characterization of the human problem as one of ignorance (*avidyā*). Ignorance is likened to a form of blindness that prevents us from seeing what is just before our eyes. Overcoming ignorance, which is the attainment of liberation (*moksha*) is akin to the regaining of sight and wisdom is described as earth's highest purifier (Bhagavadgita 3:38). The indispensability of wisdom for liberation, in other words, adds significance to the necessity and value for sharing.

Although the infinite God is the true end of all human longing, the fullness of being that all seek, the tradition has admitted consistently that God transcends all limited human efforts at definition and description. The Taittirīya Upanishad (2.9.1) speaks of the Infinite as "that from which all words, along with the mind, turn back, having failed to grasp."[6] The Kena Upanishad (2:3) expresses the impossibility of comprehending the infinite as one does a limited object by delighting in the language of paradox:

> It is known to him to whom It is unknown; he does not know It to whom It is Known. It is unknown to those who know well, and known to those who do not know.

The point of such texts is not to demean human language or to negate its value, but to remind us of its limits and of our limits in relation to God. It is a central Hindu conviction that our words are inadequate and that the One is always more than we could define, describe or understand with our finite minds. A God whose nature and essence could be fully revealed in our words or who could be contained within the boundaries of our minds would not be the One proclaimed in our traditions. This recognition of the intrinsic human limitation in attaining or formulating a complete knowledge of God means that no intellectual, theological or iconic representation is ever full and final. Each struggles to grasp and express that which is ultimately inexpressible and each attempt reflects and is influenced by the cultural and historical conditions under which it occurs.[7] Our traditions are *darśanas*, ways of seeing and understanding, but in relation to the limitlessness of the One, we cannot claim fullness of knowledge.

If it is impossible to confine the One within the boundaries of our religion or to represent it entirely through the language of our theologies, we must be open to the possibility of meaningful insights from others that may open our hearts and minds to the inexhaustible and multifaceted nature of the divine. Our confession of the limits of human understanding and language provide a powerful justification for relationships of mutual sharing and humility with people of other faiths and no faith.

Against this background, we can appreciate the voice of MK Gandhi as a Hindu-based appeal for sharing wisdom:

> I believe in the truth of all religions of the world. And since my youth upward, it has been a humble but persistent effort on my part to understand the truth of all the religions of the world, and adopt and assimi-

late in my own thought, word, and deed all that I have found to be best in those religions. The faith that I profess not only permits me to do so but renders it obligatory for me to take the best from whatever source it may come.[8]

I hold it the duty of every cultured man or woman to read sympathetically the scriptures of the world. If we are to respect others' religions as we would have them to respect our own, a friendly study of the world's religions is a sacred duty.[9]

Having highlighted the Hindu value for wisdom and for the mutual sharing of wisdom, it is important to acknowledge that certain orthodox groups have prescribed boundaries that are intended to limit access to the study of sacred texts, especially the Vedas. Eligibility for the study of the Vedas was limited to male members of the first three castes (Brahmins, Kshatriyas, and Vaishyas). Women and persons belonging to the fourth caste (Shudras) were excluded, as well as untouchables who were without caste. The entitlement to Vedic study required investiture with the sacred thread (*upanayanam*) and this ritual was available only to male members of the upper castes. Although this exclusion has been challenged and contested by various Hindu reform movements, orthodox groups still limit the sacred thread ceremony to upper caste males and the study of sacred texts is still largely in the hands of male Brahmins.

HOW DO WE SHARE?

Although there is a need, today, for a formal and explicit rejection of the eligibility for wisdom that is based on caste and gender considerations, the Hindu tradition has identified other universal considerations that define the appropriate context and methods for sharing wisdom. These are clearly articulated in a famous Muṇḍaka Upanishad text (1.2.12–13).

> A reflective person, after examining worldly gains achieved through action, understands that the uncreated cannot be created by finite action, and becomes detached.
>
> To understand that (the uncreated), he should go, with sacrificial twigs in hand, to a teacher who knows the Vedas and who is established in the infinite (*brahman*).
>
> To that student who approaches in the proper manner, whose mind is calm and who is endowed with self-control, the wise teacher should fully impart the knowledge of *brahman*, through which one knows the true and imperishable Person.[10]

First, wisdom is meaningful in the context of a specific understanding and definition of the human problem. Wisdom speaks relevantly to the reflective person who has examined life's experiences and discovered that finite or created ends such as wealth, power, fame or pleasure leave us unfulfilled. The finite fails to satisfy, not merely because it is finite and hence subject to time and change, but also because underlying every finite quest is a longing for the uncreated infinite. This grasp of the limits of human action causes what the text refers to as an attitude of detachment.

The awakening to this human problem is itself a mark of wisdom. Although such an awakening is likely to cause despair, it is a moment of opportunity. The wisdom teachings of the tradition will not speak meaningfully to the person who has not existentially reflected upon the limits of finite accomplishments. Such a person alone is a ready for the gift of wisdom (*vidyā dāna*) and this is signified by the initiative that he takes to approach a teacher.

Second, wisdom is properly transmitted in a specific relationship. The relationship here is between teacher and student. The qualified teacher of wisdom is one who knows the sacred texts and teaching methods and whose life's vision is centered on the infinite. A teacher who is well versed in the scripture, but has not grasped the immediacy of *brahman*, will transmit merely words. One who is centered in the infinite, but is not versed in the scriptural tradition will not be familiar with the methods necessary for effective teaching. Wisdom is fruitful when shared by a qualified teacher to a receptive student. Hindus regard teachers of wisdom, as well as parents and guests, with profound respect and students are enjoined to honor them in ways that are similar to the honor accorded to the divine (Taittirīya Upanishad 1.11.3). A teacher shares the gift of wisdom without any expectation of personal reward in accord with the scriptural commendation of the gift "which is made to one from whom no return is expected, with the feeling that it is one's duty to give and which is given in proper time and place and to a worthy person."[11] Inferior gifts are made with the hope of return, reluctantly, contemptuously and to unworthy persons.

Third, wisdom is liberative and fruitful in a heart and mind that are sensitive to ethical values and enjoy a certain mental and emotional disposition. The verse above from the Muṇḍaka Upanishad describes the student as calm in mind and endowed with self-control. "The knower of *brahman*," as Muṇḍaka Upanishad (3.2.9) states it, "becomes *brahman*." In the matter of knowing *brahman*, knowing is synonymous with being. One shares the nature of that which one seeks to know and so the instrument of knowledge, the mind, must conform to the object of knowledge. A seeker of wisdom must restrain the extrovert tendency of the mind and turn its attention inward. The divine is the self of all and the consequence of such an understanding, as the Bhagavadgita (6:29) puts it, is to see "the self present in all beings and all beings in the self." One grows to regard to the sufferings and joys of others as one's own and becomes active in promoting the well-being of others. A life of virtue is both the means as well as the expression of wisdom. As the Kaṭha Upanishad (2:24) puts it, "One who has not abstained from evil conduct, whose senses are not controlled and whose mind is not concentrated and calm cannot gain the Self through wisdom."[12]

RESPONSIBLE SHARING

Specifying the appropriate context and methods for sharing wisdom implies that the Hindu tradition has also noted inappropriate and irresponsible ways of sharing. One of the central concerns of the Bhagavadgita is that inappropriate sharing and, just as important, inappropriate personal example, results in a spirituality of inaction and world-withdrawal. It enjoins the one who is sharing to avoid diligently this danger.

> As the unwise act from selfish attachment to action, O Bharata, so should the wise act without selfish attachment intent on the good of the world.
>
> Let not the wise person confuse the unwise who are attached to selfish action; by devotion to action, the wise should inspire others to act.[13]

The concern of the Bhagavadgita is that since spiritual wisdom implies a certain critique of self-centered activity in the world, this critique must be offered skillfully so that the result is not world-negation and renunciation of action, but an awakening to a higher and more profound motivation centered on the wellbeing of the world. An inactive teacher, intensely denouncing selfish action in the world may be perceived easily to be negativizing the world and advocating the indifference to action. One teaches as much, or even more, by one's actions as by one's words.

The final chapter of the Bhagavadgita concludes with specific instructions on appropriate and inappropriate sharing:

> This teaching is not to be shared by you with anyone who is without discipline or devotion, who has no desire to listen and who denounces Me.[14]

The implication, of course, is that discipline, devotion, interest and openness to God are necessary for appropriate sharing.

The ideal Hindu understanding of appropriate sharing is of a dialogical relationship in which respect for the other is indispensable. As Swami Vivekananda (1863–1902) said,

> I pity the Hindu who does not see the beauty in Jesus Christ's character. I pity the Christian who does not reverence the Hindu Christ. The more a man sees of himself, the less he sees of his neighbors.[15]

For the Hindu mind, a healthy appreciation and sharing across religions need not lead to conversion. As Swami Vivekananda states,

> Do I wish that the Christian would become Hindu? God forbid. Do I wish that the Hindu or Buddhist would become Christian? God forbid.

> The seed is put into the ground, and earth and air and water are placed around it. Does the seed become the earth, or the air, or the water? No. It becomes a plant. It develops after the law of its own growth, assimilates the air, the earth, and the water, converts them into plant substance, and grows into a plant. Similar is the case with religion. The Christian is not to become a Hindu or a Buddhist, nor a Hindu or a Buddhist to become a Christian. But each must assimilate the spirit of the others and yet preserve his individuality and grow according to this own law of growth.[16]

Such an understanding, however, can no longer be taken for granted, as witnessed by the fact that concerns about inappropriate sharing have resulted in the implementation of legislation by several Indian states to prohibit conversions through coercion, allurement and fraud. In the words of the Rajasthan Anti-Conversion Bill (2006), "No person shall convert or attempt to convert either directly or otherwise any person from one religion to another by the use of force, or by allurement or by any fraudulent means nor shall any person abet such conversion."

Hindu traditions are not unfamiliar with the religious motive of sharing one's conviction and persuading others about its validity. To claim otherwise is not to be faithful to important strands of Hinduism. At the same time the traditions of India evolved a certain ethos, largely unwritten, that guided the nature of their relationships and sharing with each other. The absence of institutionalization and centralization meant that there were no organized and systematic efforts to supplant different viewpoints. Discussions among the traditions that shared significant common elements and a common culture were, on the whole, dialogical and would even result in conversion to the other's viewpoint. Even so, persons with different religious commitments belonged to the same larger religio/cultural community where boundaries were flexible and permeable. There was no inherent negativization of the fact of religious diversity and the latter was seen as a natural reflection of the diversity of human nature and experience. A widely shared understanding of the limits of human reason and symbols resulted in the understanding that truth always exceeded the comprehension and description of any one tradition and justified relationships of theological humility.

As already noted, Hindus can understand well the impetus to share one's religious convictions and experiences with others since a similar impulse is commended in Hinduism. What particularly disturbs the Hindu is the evidence in some religions of what seems to be an obsession with converting the entire world, a suspicion that this is the most fundamental motive underlying all words and actions. We can all agree that meaningful faith is not awakened and nurtured thorough aggressive proselytizing or exploitation of the vulnerability of others in conditions of tragedy and need. Meaningful sharing can only occur in a context where we recognize he fact that the other is also a person of living, faith with a tradition that speaks profoundly of God, and with whom one can enter into a mutually enriching relationship of learning and enrichment. Sharing, as the Bhagavadgita instructs, should be a response to the interest of the other and with openness to his witness. The sharing of faiths cannot be done in ways that are arrogant, militant and monological. Perhaps Gandhi describes better than any other the sharing of a faith claim in his famous analogy:

> A rose does not need to preach. It simply spreads its fragrance. The fragrance is its own sermon. If it had human understanding and if it could engage a number of preachers, the preachers would not be able to sell more roses than the fragrance itself could. The fragrance of religious and spiritual life is much finer and subtler than that of a rose.[17]

SPECIFIC WISDOMS — WHAT DOES MY TRADITION HAVE TO SHARE AND RECEIVE?

As a consequence of the antiquity and interaction among India's diverse religious and cultural traditions, Hinduism has developed approaches and insights that are pluralistic in character and may be of value in communities where religious diversity is now a fact of life and a source of tension.

The different Hindu religious systems, as already noted above, are referred to as *darśhanas* (literally, ways of seeing). These different ways of seeing express diverse temporal, spatial, and cultural locations as well as diverse identities — individually and as members of groups. Diversity, in other words, is a natural and inevitable expression of the human condition and needs to be accepted as such. The classic metaphor of the five blind men who touched various parts of an elephant and described it differently articulates well this human reality. One touched the tail and described the elephant as a giant broom, while another touched the leg and described the elephant as a pillar, and so on. Each advanced a reasonable description of the elephant, but each was limited by the partiality and specificity of his own window of experience.

Along with arguments for the acceptance of religious diversity rooted in the diversity of human nature and experiences, Hindu traditions have also called attention to the limits of human language. God is always more than can be defined, described or understood with finite human mind: descriptions will, of necessity, be diverse. This is the point of the often-quoted Ṛg Veda (1.64.46) text: "The One Being the wise call by many names." The text is a comment on the finitude of all human language in relation to the absolute. In trying to describe it, language will be diverse, since the absolute exceeds all descriptions. Each word, each symbol is inadequate and reflects the historical and cultural conditions under which it occurs. The consequence is an epistemological and philosophical humility expressing itself in a theology of pluralism that can accommodate different views about God. Hinduism reminds us that our discourse about God should not be absolutized and our symbols must not be confused with the reality to which these point.

This Hindu relativization of human language and symbols in relation to an unlimited divine is a good example, I believe, of an insight that can be shared or "nuggetized" without embracing an entire Hindu worldview. Although religious traditions, on the whole, affirm the infinity of the divine, the implications of this in relation to human limits are not always prominent in discussion. Other significant teachings of the Hindu tradition may not be so easily "exportable." Examples may include the Hindu understanding of the human religious problem to be one of *avidyā* (ignorance), and its emphasis on divine immanence and on the equal and identical existence of God in all beings.

As far as learning from other traditions is concerned, Hinduism can be challenged and enriched by the efforts of other traditions to relate religious insights and teachings to the conditions of existence in human society and be inspired by efforts to transform structures of oppression and injustice. Many influential interpretations of the relationship between God and the world in the Hindu tradition result in a devaluation of the world and the meaning of life within it. The world is sometimes likened to a sense-illusion that we conjure and experience because of our ignorance of God. It is equated with *māyā*, a term that has historical overtones of illusion, deceptiveness, and untruth. The denial of reality to the world is closely connected to disclaiming its value and meaning. When the reality and value of the world is in doubt, the significance of issues within it, such as justice and equality, do not become important.

Some of the clearest examples of oppressive and unjust structures in Hindu society are those related to caste and gender. In spite of various legal measures enacted by the Indian government to prevent caste discrimination and to provide better opportunities for those who are victims, the phenomenon of untouchability persists in contemporary India and Hindus continue to define the meaning of Hindu identity over and against those who are deemed unequal and, for this reason, marginalized. The sharp distinctions between self and other, the boundaries of the pure and impure, are still drawn sharply in Indian villages, where the character of human and economic relationships are still governed by the hierarchies of caste and where reports of violence against persons of lower castes are common.

Hinduism, like other world religions that developed in patriarchal culture, reflects assumptions about male gender supremacy that have been oppressive to Hindu women. Gender injustice manifests itself in the fact that a disproportionate percentage of the illiterate in India are women, the abortion of female fetuses because of a preference for male offspring, the stigmatization of widows, and the custom of dowry that depletes the economic resources of families into which girls are born and that makes them feel guilty for being women.

In highlighting and employing the liberative resources of Hinduism to struggle against oppression, Hinduism can learn from movements in other traditions, such as Engaged Buddhism and Christian Liberation Theology, that see justice and spirituality as inseparable. These movements emphasize that the interior life of holiness and piety must find outward expression in a passion for justice. These two dimensions of authentic spirituality mutually nourish and are incomplete without each other. Without the concern for justice, personal piety becomes obsessively self-centered. At the same time, attentiveness to and cultivation of the interior spiritual life nourish and provide the motivation for the work of justice. Mutual religious sharing on these issues can be immensely beneficial.

ON FORGIVENESS AND LOVE

One of the central insights of the Hinduism, as noted above, consistently proclaimed by its diverse traditions, is the unity of all existence in God. God is envisioned as the common and unifying reality in all created beings. The Hindu tradition understands God to be the one truth in each one of us, uniting us with each other and with all things.

The non-dual tradition of Hinduism (Advaita) articulates the most radical doctrine of the unity of existence in its denial of any ontological dualism and in its view that reality is not two. *Brahman*, the infinite, constitutes the essential nature of all that exists and is present in all beings as the very ground of selfhood (*ātman*). The discerning person therefore, sees herself in all and all in herself. This Advaita teaching may be thought of as the spiritual parallel to the belief of science that life, in its totality, descended from a single cell. The cells of all living things share a basic similarity, including the same DNA code and similar amino acids. Science suggests a common origin and nature for the countless expressions of life.

The significance that Hinduism grants to the truth of life's unity may be appreciated from the fact that its discernment is considered to the hallmark of wisdom and liberation. We are invited to recognize the equality and identity of the divine in ourselves and in all beings. The Bhagavadgita (18:20) commends the knowledge that enables a person to see, "one imperishable Being in all beings, undivided in separate beings." A false and inferior way of seeing reality is to regard existing things as isolated, separate and independent of each other and to see in all beings "separate entities of various kinds" (18:21). We are not to deny the uniqueness of individuals, communities and cultures, but affirm the fundamental unity that underlies all. This Hindu understanding of life's unity is the justification of its regard for the entire world as a single family (*vasudhaiva kutumbakam*). It is also the source of its core values such as *ahiṁsā* (non-injury), *dayā* (compassion) and *dāna* (generosity). Compassion is an integral expression of the vision of life's unity and fundamental interelatedness.

The Hindu understanding of life's unity is all-inclusive. No one can be excluded, since the divine, who constitutes the unifying truth, does not exclude anyone and anything. "God," as the Bhagavadgita (13:28) puts it, "abides equally in all beings." This is the Hindu antidote to our human tendency to deny the personhood, worth and dignity of the other. It is from the perspective of life's unity that we question exploitative and unjust human relationships, which foster conflict, and divisiveness and it is the same perspective, which urges us to cross boundaries and work for forgiveness and reconciliation. If our world is indeed a single family (*vasudhaiva kutumbakam*), both spiritually and biologically, the quality of our relationships should reflect the moral and ethical implications of this truth. Īśa Upanishad (6) reminds us that the wise person who beholds all beings in the self and the self in all beings is liberated from hate. From the profundity of the Hindu understanding of the nature of life's unity, estrangement from another is estrangement from one's own self and the hate of the other is the hate of one's self. To be in conflict with another is also to be in conflict with one's self. To inflict suffering on another is to violate one's own self.

The Hindu tradition assumes that a person who is truly grasped by the truth of life's unity in God will find delight in unselfishly striving for the well-being of others. Ignorance of life's unity, on the other hand, expresses itself in greed, ego-centeredness, and the readiness to inflict suffering on others through reckless exploitation. This is the reason why the traditions of Hinduism have almost uniformly described the fundamental human problem to be one of ignorance or, in Sanskrit, *avidyā*. Human conflict and suffering are rooted in a fundamental misunderstanding of the nature of reality. Ignorance can be overcome and when it is and when we are awakened to the truth of life's unity in the divine, there will be a corresponding transformation in the quality of our relationships.

The view that the human problem at its most fundamental level is one of ignorance and that this ignorance expresses itself in our failure to discern the unity of all existence is central to the development of a Hindu approach to forgiveness, and reconciliation. It enables us to see the other, the one with whom we disagree and with who we may be locked in struggle, as a fellow human being. We cannot dehumanize the one in whom we see ourselves or long for his or her humiliation. This approach was at the heart of the Gandhian philosophy and practice of non-violent resistance (*satyagraha*). Even in the midst of the strongest disagreements, Gandhi never sought to win support for his case by demonizing his opponent. He understood clearly that when a conflict is constructed sharply in terms of we and they, victory and defeat, the doors to reconciliation and a transformed community are shut. One is left with an enemy, a defeated enemy perhaps, and the next round of the conflict is only postponed. Gandhi included the opponent in the circle of his identity.

In restraining a disciple from a desire for revenge and violence, the saintly Hindu teacher, Ramana Maharishi, asked a provocative question. "If your teeth suddenly bite your tongue, do you knock them out in consequence?" Ramana's question implies the truth of life's unity as well as the reality of ignorance. The teeth and tongue are part of the same body and the biting, however, painful, is more in the nature of an error. The consequence is a disposition to understanding and compassion, without which reconciliation is impossible.

Belief in ignorance as the source of suffering disposes one to an attitude of forgiveness since it orients one to look beyond the immediate action to its underlying causes. We are more likely to respond with hate when we believe that those who hurt us have done so because of intentional malevolence. If we see the action as rooted in ignorance and a flawed understanding of reality, our attitude to the other will be compassionate. We are liberated from hate, bitterness and the desire to inflict pain on the other and we are open to reconciliation.

> The conduct of the good to the wicked is similar to that of the sandal tree to the axe,—for the fragrant sandal gives its perfume to the axe that cuts it. For this reason, sandal-wood is loved and desired by all and enjoys the honor of being applied on the heads of divine icons.[18]

One of the finest examples of the practice of such an approach occurs in the Ramayana of Valmiki. After the defeat of Ravana, Hanuman sought the permission of Sita to destroy the female servants of Ravana who had guarded and taunted her during her imprisonment. Sita, however, saw them as victims like her and offered the superior ideal of forgiveness and reconciliation. "Who would be angry," asks Sita, "with women who are dependent on a monarch who is their superior and who act on other's advice as mere servants or slaves? I wish in compassion to protect the slaves of Ravana." Forgiveness and compassion are attributes of the divine in Hinduism.

> A superior being does not render evil for evil, this is a maxim one should observe; the ornament of virtuous persons is their conduct. One should never harm the wicked or the good or even criminals meriting death. A noble soul will ever exercise compassion towards even those who enjoy injuring others or those of cruel deeds when they are actually committing them—for who is without fault?[19]

THE HINDU TEMPLE OF
MAPLE GROVE, MINNESOTA

A contemporary application of Hindu principles of forgiveness can be seen in how one community responded to hate crimes. On April 5, 2006, just months before it was scheduled for a grand opening, the new Hindu Temple in Maple Grove, Minnesota was viciously attacked. In the stillness and obscurity of darkness, vandals broke into the building, bashed walls and windows and, most painfully for the Hindu community, smashed sacred icons (*murtis*) that were awaiting ritual installation on the altar. The scene was one of devastation and brought tears to heart and eyes of who visited the temple during the days following the destruction. The new temple was over thirty years in the making and a source of pride to all. The damage was estimated to be over $200,000.

After a persistent police investigation and the offer of a monetary reward by the Hindu Temple, two young men, ages nineteen and twenty were arrested for the crime. They quickly confessed and a date was set for sentencing. On the day of sentencing, a Hindu Temple representative, Dr, Shashikant Sane, appeared and spoke on behalf of the young men. Speaking against the ethic of "an eye for an eye," Dr. Sane, pleaded for a light sentence and the opportunity for the young men to become good and productive citizens and not hardened criminals in the prison system. In the view of the Hindu community, the problem of the young men as one of ignorance and not one of evil. Hennepin County District Judge, Kevin Burke agreed. Burke confessed that he had been inclined to give a sixty-day jail sentence to both men, but, on account of the plea from the Hindu community, he sentenced them to serve thirty days in prison and to pay restitution of $96,454.

On August 27, 2006, prior to their sentencing, the two youths returned to the temple to seek the forgiveness of the Hindu community. They were welcomed and greeted with hugs, a meal, and teachings about basic Hindu values such as self-control and non-violence. The purpose of their visit to the temple, representatives explained, was not to shame or humiliate them. Hindus acknowledged that the young men were also suffering as a consequence of what they had done and that the purpose of the visit was to help healing on both sides. Speaking to the young men during their visit to the temple, Dr. Sane said, "Karma is the law of cause and effect by which each individual creates his own destiny. We divide between evil and evildoers. Your actions were inappropriate, and you're responsible for those actions. That, I cannot stop. But as human beings, you are nothing but divine. You can make the right choices and achieve the potential that God has bestowed upon you."[20]

NOTES

1. See *Rāmacaritamānasa*, trans. R. C. Prasad (Delhi: Motilal Banarsidass, 1991), 478–79. Rama is identified by Tulasidasa with God and presented as a divine incarnation (*avatara*).
2. My translation.
3. *The Bhagavadgita*, trans. S. Radhakrishnan (New York: Harper & Row, 1973).
4. My translation.
5. See also *Bhagavadgita* 10:20 and 18:61.
6. See *Upanishads*, trans. Patrick Olivelle (New York: Oxford University Press, 1996).
7. Although the limits of human understanding in relation to divine are noted in Hindu sacred texts, the implication of this insight for learning from others is not always articulated.
8. M. K. Gandhi, *The Voice of Truth* (Ahmedabad: Navajivan Publishing House, 1969), 264–65.
9. M. K. Gandhi, *The Voice of Truth*, 267.
10. My translation.
11. *Bhagavadgita* 17:20.
12. My translation.
13. *Bhagavadgita* 3:25–26. My translation.
14. *Bhagavadgita* 18, 67.
15. This excerpt is from a lecture delivered by Vivekananda on "Christianity in India," in Detroit, on March 11, 1894. *Collected Works of Swami Vivekananda*, 13th ed., vol. 8 (Calcutta: Advaita Ashrama, 1970), 219.
16. *The Complete Works of Swami Vivekananda*, vol. 1, 13.
17. From an address to foreign missionaries, *Young India*, 23-4-'31 found on http://www.mkgandhi.org/.
18. Sri Rāmacharitamānasa, trans. R. C. Prasad (Delhi: Motilal Banarsidass, 1991). Author's translation. These are the opening words of Rama, in the Rāmacharitamānasa of Tulasidasa, in response to a question asking him to clarify the differences between the virtuous and evil human beings.
19. *The Ramayana of Valmiki*, vol. 3, trans., Hari Prasad Shastri (London: Shanti Sadan, 1959), 331–32. These words were spoken by Sita, in the Ramayana, in response to Hanuman who wanted to slay the servants of Ravana who imprisoned and tortured her in Lanka.
20. For more information about the Maple Grove temple vandalism and its aftermath, see "Two Teens Held for Vandalising Minnesota Temple," *Rediff India Abroad*, May 24, 2006, http://www.rediff.com/news/2006/may/24temple.htm and "Update: Two Men Plead Guilty to Vandalism of Maple Grove Hindu Temple, *The Pluralism Project*, July 10, 2006, http://pluralism.org/news/update-two-men-plead-guilty-to-vandalism-of-maple-grove-hindu-temple/.

THREE
A Sikh Perspective

Pal Ahluwalia

WHAT IS WISDOM?

There is a significant difference between one who has acquired knowledge and one who is wise. We know of people who are intellectually brilliant but who lack the capacity to engage beyond their particular area of specialization. And yet, we know of people who are not renowned for their intellectual brilliance but who have an understanding and wisdom that seems beyond mere intellect. These individuals are often characterized as having character, virtue, and insight. They are able to cut through to the core of complexity with elegant simplicity.

Wisdom is the ability to know that which is of the deepest significance. This "knowing" comes not through mental calculation or shrewdness but rather through what we may call "intuition." This form of knowing is about an inner experience, an inner knowing that is embodied within us. Such wisdom is manifest within us and can be harnessed or awakened through prayer, meditation, service, and contemplation. It is, in short, an inner form of knowing. This form of knowledge cannot simply be acquired through reading books but entails an experiential element.[1]

> You may read and read loads of books; you may read and study vast multitudes of books.
> You may read and read boat-loads of books; you may read and read and fill pits with them.
> You may read them year after year; you may read them as many months as there are.
> You may read them all your life; you may read them with every breath.

> O Nanak, only one thing is of any account: everything else is useless babbling and idle talk in ego (Sri Guru Granth Sahib [SGGS Ji], 467).[2]
> Wisdom cannot be found through mere words. To explain it is as hard as iron.
> When the Lord bestows His Grace, then alone it is received; other tricks and orders are useless (SGGS Ji, 465).

Wisdom in Sikhi[3] is about experiencing the Creator and creation. At some level, it is about knowing the Divine plan, while at the same time realising the impossibility to fully knowing the infinite or indeed His plan. This is precisely because of the impossibility of human description of the Creator. At its core, in Sikhi wisdom entails realising and experiencing God as described by Guru Nanak Dev Ji (the founding Guru) in the opening lines of the Sri Guru Granth Sahib Ji (henceforth: SGGS), the *mul mantar*:

> God is One, Manifest as Word, True of Name, Creative Being, Without Fear, Without Enmity, Whose Form is Infinite, Self-Existent, through the grace of the guru.
> True in the beginning, True before time began,
> He is True, Nanak, and ever will be True. (SGGS Ji,1)

In Sikhi, *gun* is understood as virtues or good qualities. The importance of *gun* is made clear by Guru Nanak Dev Ji who declares categorically that "devotion without virtues is impossible" (SGGS Ji, 4). Virtues, according to the Gurus, can be learnt and inculcated through interaction with those who are virtuous. As Guru Nanak Dev Ji puts it, "In the society of the holy, one becomes holy, and one runs after virtues, forsaking one's sins" (SGGS Ji, 414). In this regard, the acquisition of *gun* leads to wisdom, which plays a key role in Sikh ethics.[4] The terms to denote wisdom and the fact that one is wise are respectively *gian* and *giani*.[5] Nevertheless, two other terms *budhi* (intelligence) and *bibek budhi* (wisdom) are also used to convey the difference between mere intelligence and wisdom. Critically, one can only acquire *bibek budhi* through the grace of the Guru.

According to Guru Nanak Dev Ji, the spiritual seeker is expected to contemplate the real nature of knowledge under the guidance of a spiritual leader. In the quest for spiritual realization, one reaches beyond oneself and the egocentric reasoning (*budhi*) is transformed into a discriminating reason (*bibek budhi*) that seeks metaphysical reality. In short, in Sikhi, reason is implied in the very notion of *gian*. As Sher Singh points out, "in moving from intellect to intuition, we are not moving in the direction of unreason, but are getting into the deepest rationality of which human nature is capable"[6]

In the opening composition of the SGGS Ji, the "Japji Sahib," Guru Nanak Dev Ji points out that wisdom is "a comprehensive point of view as indicated in the actions of a person."[7] He maps out what wisdom is and how it can be acquired in three steps. These include: *suniye* (hearing), *manne* (reflecting) and *dhian* (meditation). These steps are clarified further in the Japji Sahib with four stanzas devoted to hearing. First, it is made clear that a person should hear about the lives of exalted persons as well as various aspects of the world. Second, a seeker should hear the contents of consciousness within themselves. Such hearing expands the very consciousness of the seeker. Third, the seeker is implored to hear about fundamental moral qualities that must be cultivated. Finally, the seeker hears about the practical application of the wisdom of leaders and learns how these leaders helped others and guided others during difficult times.

In essence, hearing is meant to teach one about creation and recognizing a higher consciousness in all as well as realizing that certain moral principles and their practical application can be witnessed in the lives of those who have lived wisely and who similarly guide others. But simply hearing is for Guru Nanak Dev Ji not enough. For this entails merely accepting what one hears. On the contrary, one is called to reflect on what one has heard. As such, *manne* or reflection is the second step toward wisdom and once again it is elaborated in four stanzas in the Japji Sahib.

First, Guru Nanak Dev Ji points out that it is impossible to describe the entire process of reflection, primarily because the process itself is vast and infinite. Nevertheless, he tells us that it is through such reflection that the mind, awareness, and intellect are shaped and sharpened. Second, it is through reflection that one is able to realise the true nature of reality. Third, reflection removes all hindrances from the path of a seeker and bestows upon one great honour. Critically, the person endowed with such reflection becomes deeply aware of the social context and seeks to serve the Creator and creation. Finally, through reflection one realises salvation itself. It is at this point that altruism becomes central. This is necessarily so, because one realises that the same spirit pervades all creation and all of humanity is simply part of one family.

The third aspect of wisdom is *dhian*, which can be translated as a process of meditation and inner reflection. It is the synthesis of the knowledge that one acquires from *suniye* (hearing) and *manne* (reflection). This synthesis is itself constituent of *gian* or wisdom. The virtue of wisdom synthesizes knowledge of the world as well as spiritual knowledge. A great deal of importance is attached to practice as an essential constituent of wisdom. It is through the repetition of the *nam*, (name) as well as in service to all creation that one attains wisdom. This wisdom does not necessarily require the knowledge of texts but is attainable only through the quelling of the ego.

What is clear is that wisdom is at the behest of the Creator who can give it as a blessing instantly to anyone He so chooses—for it is up to Him to make "angels out of mere people":

> A hundred times a day, I am a sacrifice to my Guru;

He made angels out of men, without delay. (SGGS Ji, 462)

Furthermore, an inflated ego obstructs the path to liberation by standing in opposition to anything that is "other":

> Oh Nanak, freedom's gate is tight,
> The very small alone can pass.
> When ego's swollen up the mind,
> How can it hope to pass that gate?
> It's when the guru comes to us
> That ego goes and all is light
> At last this soul finds its release
> And always stays absorbed in bliss. (SGGS Ji, 509)

Guru Nanak Dev Ji goes on to say that, "Rare in the world is the man of wisdom who reflects on wisdom and rare is the wise man in this world who practices this wisdom" (SGGS Ji, 413). In a similar vein, Bhagat Kabir Ji points out that, "if you have wisdom, destroy your evil and discipline your body" (SGGS Ji, 342). These quotations reinforce the point that wisdom can only be obtained when the ego is negated. As Guru Nanak Dev Ji explains, "How can one instruct the one who says that he knows? He who considers himself as having crossed the sea, how can one tell him?" (SGGS Ji, 938).

WHY SHARE WISDOM?

In Sikhi, wisdom results only from fusion—the merging of the self and the Divine. The one who attains this wisdom is a *Brahm-Giani*, one who has attained the ultimate knowledge and wisdom as outlined above. Guru Arjan Dev Ji defines the *Brahm-Giani* as one who has the True Being in mind, the True One on the tongue and perceives none other than the One. Furthermore, the *Brahm-Giani* always yearns to do good for others as a *parupkari* (SGGS Ji, 273; 816). The attaining of this state of *Brahm-Giani* represents the very embodiment of Godly traits. These traits or *gun* include the need for one to be kind, forgiving, compassionate, truthful, unselfish, humble, pure, just, fearless, merciful, generous, and loving—all of which are essential ingredients if one is to be attuned to God. In *Sukhmani Sahib*, Guru Arjan Dev Ji gives us an insight into the *Brahm-Giani*:

> The Brahm-Giani is the purest of the pure;
> Like water to which filth cannot remain attached
> The mind of the Brahm-Giani is enlightened with divine light;
> Like the firmament over the earth (which is present everywhere).
> To the Brahm-Giani friends and foes are alike;
> As he has no pride.
> The Brahm-Giani is the most exalted of the exalted;
> (Yet) he treats himself to be most humble in his mind.
> Only those are Brahm-Gianis;

Guru Nanak says, whom God makes so. (SGGS Ji, 272)

In their love for God and His creation, it is natural for the *Brahm-Gianis* to want to share these virtues. As the Guru points out, "Yes, share we should the virtues with our friends and shed our sins" (SGGS Ji, 766). Clearly, embedded in the notion of the sharing of these virtues there is an aspect of sharing socially.

All species carry within them a spark of life that emanates from the infinite divine flame—that is, the Creator. The Guru Granth Sahib Ji tells us to recognise that there is only one God as well as the commonality of the human race. As Bhagat Kabir Ji notes:

> First, Allah created the Light; then, by His Creative Power, He made all mortal beings.
> From the One Light, the entire universe welled up. So who is good, and who is bad?
> O people, O Siblings of Destiny, do not wander deluded by doubt.
> The Creation is in the Creator, and the Creator is in the Creation, totally pervading and permeating all places.
> The clay is the same, but the Fashioner has fashioned it in various ways.
> There is nothing wrong with the pot of clay—there is nothing wrong with the Potter.
> The One True Lord abides in all; by His making, everything is made.
> Whoever realizes the Hukam of His Command, knows the One Lord. He alone is said to be the Lord's slave.
> The Lord Allah is Unseen; He cannot be seen. The Guru has blessed me with this sweet molasses.
> Says Kabir, my anxiety and fear have been taken away; I see the Immaculate Lord pervading everywhere. (SGGS Ji, 1340)

The SGGS Ji is adamant about religious pluralism. In an infinite context, all revelations of the Divine are valid and hence it is stated that no single religion (including Sikhi) can claim to be the full and final expression of God because of the inexhaustible and infinite nature of God's attributes as well as the relativity of the modes of perception. Guru Nanak Dev Ji metaphorically captures this by saying that the "brave sees God in the form of the Might, the intellectual comprehends Him in the form of the Light (of knowledge), the aesthete perceives the Divine in His aspects of Beauty, and the moralist envisions Him as Goodness."[8]

Life on this globe fits within a spiritual scale that ranges from pure matter to pure spirit in an ascending scale. Pure matter is at the lower end of the scale and is followed by vegetation, the animal kingdom, humans, and pure spirit at the pinnacle representing the Creator. As humans, we are bestowed with the power of reasoning for differentiating between good and evil (which have co-existed since creation itself). The human being sits at the apex of this evolutionary scale and, because of the capacity to reason, is required and expected to support and protect creation, which has been entrusted to us. Furthermore, the human being has a duty toward fellow beings. It would be wrong to condemn fellow beings, as well as creatures at the lower end of the spiritual scale, because humility and forgiveness are the bedrock of spirituality. It is incumbent for the human to be forgiving, compassionate, loving, kind, and humble within all creation. We are not on this planet to pursue selfish interests. There is a higher motive demanded from us all. Our intended primary aim is prayer, contemplation, and service to others, which leads us ultimately to be reunited with the Lord. Sikhi requires one to be an integral part of the world, not a recluse or hermit.

Sikh ethics then are fundamentally about one's duty and responsibility not simply to the Creator but to all of creation. Sikhi emerged in a context where it was surrounded by Hinduism and Islam and the message of the Sikh Gurus was aimed at all of humanity. The ethical relationship is one that hinges on the responsibility one has to the other. The "other" here has a double meaning, signifying all the species that inhabit the planet as well as the infinite "Other" who is always omnipresent yet difficult, indeed impossible, to comprehend, being attainable only once the self is transcended. This recognition necessarily imbibes a need for sharing.

Sharing then becomes an essential part of Sikhi because altruism is a necessary prerequisite for serving the Creator and creation. It is through sharing that one begins to appreciate the key Godly trait of selflessness. Nevertheless, it is important to note that it is only through love that one can realize God. As the tenth Guru put it: "All should listen to this truth that only those who love God can realize Him."[9]

The overarching commonality of humanity demands that we share our spiritual and worldly earnings. Furthermore, once the ego has been quelled, it is easy to see how all that is given to an individual belongs to God and that this entails a responsibility to share. Fareed Ji, one of the Muslim Saints whose writings are enshrined in the Sri Guru Granth Sahib Ji, implores:

> If you are wise, be simple;
> If you are powerful, be weak;
> And when there is nothing to share, then share with others. (SGGS Ji, 1384)

Here, Fareed Ji is suggesting that it is only possible to share when one's ego has been negated and when one truly believes that he or she has nothing to share because all that there is belongs to God. It is only then that "true" sharing can be effected.

HOW DO WE SHARE?

The best way to share is explained by Guru Nanak Dev Ji who advocated a threefold motto which is seen as analogous to the essence of Sikhi:

1. *Naam Japo*—meditate on God (*Simran*)—and you will become wise (*mat uchi*).
2. *Kirat Karo*—earn your living through remembrance of God and hard work. Only then can work be worship—live in the Lord's presence.
3. *Wand Ke Chhako*—earn an honest living and share your spiritual and worldly earnings with humanity. Serve God and creation (*Sewa*)—you will become humble (*man neeva*).[10]

The first two principals are important for attaining wisdom, but the third, *wand de chako*, is the key to how one should share. Furthermore, these fundamental principles can only be practised effectively if one has love for God and His creation. They are a means to ameliorate and polish our human intelligence, *budhi* into *bibek budhi* (wisdom). In terms of *kirat karo*, Sikhi attaches a great deal of importance to the notion of truthful living as emphasised by the SGGS Ji that "truth is high, higher still is truthful living." According to Sikhi, wisdom cannot be attained without ethical activity namely—*simran* and *sewa*. Nevertheless, all three are inseparable, and it is not possible to discuss them in isolation. By following this threefold motto one can attain mystical awareness of the Truth which according to the SGGS Ji is attained with utmost devotion, faith and love. The way to share is to accept three conditions:

1. The acceptance of the presence of God as the wisest of the wise;
2. To always live in the presence of God; and
3. To live within a connected infinite spiritual scale.

By living a life imbued with these conditions, one is blessed and rendered accountable and responsive to the needs of God's creation, which entails both a duty and a responsibility. This demands an ethical way to live whereby *wand ke chako* becomes a central tenet of the practice of everyday life. However, to treat this merely as an obligation is to miss the point that love is the overarching prerequisite to any form of sharing.

Why is Love a Requirement for Gaining True Wisdom?

When sharing is approached from such a stance of love, the very idea of not sharing is incomprehensible. Sharing has to occur as a mutual exchange through dialogue, engagement and prayer. It is imperative that we give without expecting anything in return. And, above all, one must not be frugal when sharing. As Guru Nanak explains in order to share it is essential that, "I dedicate my body, mind, wealth and all to Him. I totally sacrifice my soul to Him" (SGGS Ji, 47).

SPECIFIC WISDOMS—WHAT DOES MY TRADITION HAVE TO SHARE AND RECEIVE?

The threefold motto of Guru Nanak Dev Ji discussed above is an important wisdom that Sikhi has to offer. This is perhaps best exemplified through the Sikh practice of serving *langar* (blessed food). Guru Nanak Dev Ji inaugurated the practice of *langar* when his father gave him twenty rupees to start a business. Contrary to his father's expectations and much to his consternation, Guru Nanak Dev Ji spent this money on serving food to sacred and holy people. This profound eternal act became known as *Sacha Sodha*—the righteous transaction. Since then, *langar* has become the cornerstone of Sikh religious practices and embodies that very ethos today.

Langar is an institution that serves blessed food unconditionally to all. What differentiates *langar* from other acts of providing food is that it is served twenty-four hours a day all year round. The idea that there are set meal times such as lunch and dinner is irrelevant at the Gurudwara (Sikh place of worship), because any hour is a mealtime. *Langar* is a community kitchen that above all else is a labour of love and an integral part of both service to the Almighty as well as to God's creation. The threefold motto of *naam japo, kirat karo* and *wand ke chhako* is embodied within the practice of *langar*, which throughout all its stages, is linked inextricably with prayer. It is to be financed through one's honest living and shared amongst all. It is not only a benevolent and charitable act but is meant to embody humility, equality and love for all those involved in its preparation, its serving as well as its consumption.

A living example of this tradition was the serving of *langar* carried out by the Sikh community at the 2004 Council for a Parliament of the World's Religions in Barcelona. What was remarkable here was not that the Sikhs served *langar*, rather, what was more important was the effect of this profound act. It led to people of all faiths coming together to engage in the preparation, and the serving *langar* and in the cleaning up process. In Barcelona, *langar* was no longer just a Sikh institution; it became a concrete way of sharing—an example of how faiths give and receive from each other in a responsible manner.

Receiving is also an integral part of Sikhi. Indeed, the very definition of a Sikh is a "learner" and, as such, learning is a lifetime pursuit. The greatest example of receiving in the Sikh faith is the equal status that is accorded to the writings of Hindu and Muslim saints. The Guru Granth Sahib Ji is a Divine, revealed, sacred Scripture that was compiled by the Gurus for all of humanity. Guru Granth Sahib Ji is a perfect example of interfaith harmony comprising the verses of the Gurus as well as Hindu and Muslim Saints whose writings correspond with the teachings of the Sikh Gurus. Significantly, the teachings of these Muslim and Hindu Saints are accorded the same status as that of the Gurus. This is further evidence of the Sikh belief about the commonality of all humanity. It forces them to recognise that within the infinite context there are countless possibilities.

For example, the crucifixion of Christ is as perfect an example of compassion as there is, and Sikhs have much to receive from understanding the power and love of that act. Most importantly, as a lifelong learner, a Sikh has a responsibility to learn from anyone that has the capacity to teach. This necessitates adopting a critical stance and an ethical position which allow Sikhs to engage with others in non-coercive, non-dominative and non-essentialist ways. This means that in order to share responsibly Sikhs do not have the right to impose their particular teachings but also that they have to be particularly vigilant of the right of other traditions to freely practice their faiths. It was in this context that the ninth Guru, Guru Tegh Bhadhur Ji, sacrificed his life in order that the Hindus who were being persecuted by the Mughal Empire could freely practice their faith. In short, he personified the very principle of parupkari, the yearning for doing good for others.

SHARING WISDOMS—LOVE AND FORGIVNESS

Sikhi's most profound precept is love. In this paper, it has been suggested often that acquiring wisdom requires one to love both God and the entire creation. And, it is precisely this love that necessitates that one shares wisdom not as an obligation but as a gift, an unconditional gift, for which one does not expect to receive anything in return. The SGGS Ji is full of references to the love-relationship between *bhakta* (devotee) and *prabhu* (the gracious and loving Lord), which is essentially a spiritual experience of union between the two.

This is akin to the Sikh marriage ceremony or the *Lavan*, the circumambulation of the Sri Guru Granth Sahib Ji, whilst reciting four passages that suggest that a human bonding in marriage is the ground for the spiritual marriage with God. In Sikhi, humans are all feminised and God is the male who has to be wooed through love and total surrender. According to the Sikh Gurus, spiritual love is the concentration of our total being in love. Sheikh Farid for whom "greed is the negation of love" portrays God as the "sweet, loving, compassionate, provident, master, magnanimous, and beloved."[11] However, loving and serving God is only one part of the prescription, whereas to love and serve humanity is the other complementary part. Hence, the love of God and the love of people are both important as Guru Nanak Dev Ji illustrates:

> Listen my heart:
> Let thy love be that of the lotus for the pool,
> Though the ripples shake the lotus and torment it,
> It flowers and loves even more the waters...
> Listen my heart: love God ceaselessly
> As the fish loves water...
> O my heart listen:
> Love God as water loves milk.
> The water must suffer, must evaporate
> Before the heat can touch the milk.[12]

In Sikhi, God is without any enmity, malice or ill-will. God is love. He is the Lord of every being. He is merciful, compassionate and the protector of all beings. It is precisely these Godly attributes that can be adopted by humans in relation to fellow beings. Hence, just as God is friendly toward us, we should all be friendly to fellow beings (SGGS Ji, 671). It was in this context that Guru Gobind Singh Ji declared that "I recognize the entire humanity as one single race."[13]

Just as love is central to Sikhi, so is forgiveness. Sikhi recognises that as humans we are frail and prone to transgress all the time. But it is through prayer that Sikhs can seek forgiveness from the Lord who is all-loving. Forgiveness is perhaps one of the greatest spiritual gifts. It enables one to be relieved of the sorrows of the past. But it is pertinent to ask what forgiveness means. Forgiveness does not in any way justify or condone harmful actions. Rather, forgiveness entails recognising that, "Never again will I knowingly allow this to happen." Forgiveness is an opportunity to let go of pain and resentment. Guru Nanak Dev Ji has given a very appropriate place to forgiveness and says that forgiveness is good conduct and that it breeds contentment: "to imbibe the spirit of forgiveness is for me the fasting, good conduct and contentment" (SGGS Ji, 223).

The Sikh scriptures contain several textual sources that illustrate the centrality and the benefits of forgiveness. Forgiveness of the Lord is sought and shown to be a virtue. Indeed, it is made clear that to be able to forgive others, we have to forgive ourselves first, and then ask forgiveness from others for the hurt and pain caused by us to them. Asking forgiveness of others and forgiving oneself is an act of great humility and shows one's faith in God and the ability to obey the Divine mandate. Without forbearance one perishes spiritually. As Guru Nanak says: "Without forgiveness and forbearance innumerable have perished" (SGGS Ji, 937).

A good example of forgiveness can be illustrated through the parable of Bhai Joga Singh, who was unconditionally forgiven by Guru Gobind Singh Ji. From an early age, Bhai Joga Singh lived at the Guru's Darbar and was regarded as a great devotee. One day the Guru asked him his name and he replied, "O true Guru, my name is Joga Singh." The Guru asked, "Whose Joga you are?" (which can be translated "for whom are you?"). To this he replied, "I am Guru Joga (I am for the Guru)." In response, the Guru promised, "If you are Guru Joga, then Guru is tere Joga" (if you are for the Guru, then the Guru is for you).

After some time, Joga Singh went home to Peshawar to get married at the instigation of his parents. It is often recalled that when the marriage ceremony had been partly completed a man arrived with an urgent message from the Guru asking Bhai Joga Singh to return to Anandpur immediately. At once, Bhai Joga Singh left for Anandpur thereby obeying the Guru's hukam (command). During this journey, the parable recounts that his ego was hugely inflated and he thought to himself, "Who could have acted like me? Certainly very few Sikhs would carry out the Guru's order like I have." That night Bhai Joga Singh was overwhelmed by evil-passion, and he made his way to the house of a prostitute. As soon as he reached the house of the prostitute, a guard appeared and would not allow Bhai Joga Singh to enter the house. Despite repeated attempts the guard refused to allow him to enter. When he reached Anandpur, Bhai Joga Singh appeared before the Guru who reminded him of the promise that he had made many years ago. The Guru explained that the previous night he had to appear in the garb of a guard to protect him. Bhai Joga Singh fell at Guru's feet and asked for forgiveness.

This parable shows clearly that even when we transgress (which as humans we continuously do), God is all loving and forgiving. Rather than condemning Bhai Joga Singh, Guru Gobind Singh took extraordinary measures to protect his disciple. The significance for Sikhs of this parable is that they have to inculcate this very spirit of forgiveness in the practice of everyday life. The centrality of forgiveness is further illustrated in the following statements from the SGGS Ji:

> By adopting forgiveness and gathering truth, one partakes of God's name, the nectar. (261)
> Still your duality and hold fast to forgiveness. (343)
> Hold on to forgiveness in the refuge of the true Guru. (1030)
> The attributes (of a person of God) are the gathering of the riches of forgiveness. (1171)
> Where there is greed, there is death. Where there is forgiveness there is God Himself. (1372)

NOTES

1. Avtar Singh, *Ethics of the Sikhs* (Patiala: Punjabi University, 1996), 161, recalled an event that profoundly challenged him. He was visiting a Saint and when he arrived he found a large gathering that was listening attentively to subjects such as the nature of reality and our knowledge of it. The Saint, a lay seeker of knowledge, he points out, was keeping alive the urge for metaphysics. He juxtaposes this to the difficulty that he had in the classroom where he taught philosophy and Sikhi.

2. All translations are the author's own.

3. In this paper I will use the term "Sikhi" to describe the Sikh tradition, based on the recommendation of Arvind Pal Mandair, *Sikhism: A Guide for the Perplexed* (London: Bloomsbury, 2013). This choice is informed by a cluster of problems relating to language and categories. The very idea of Sikhism, the Sikh faith or the Sikh religion is a poor translation of the notion of the Sikh dharam or simply "Sikhi." Similarly, to refer to the SGGS Ji as the Sikh scriptures or the Holy text is to miss the essence of its status as a "living Guru." The problems of translation are compounded in English as a result of the gendering of language, as well as the introduction of Judeo-Christian overtones as a result of the colonial experience. See further Arvind-Pal Mandair, *Religion and the Spectre of the West* (New York: Columbia University Press, 2009).

4. On Sikh ethics see Surindar Singh Kholi, *Sikh Ethics* (New Delhi: Munshiram Manoharlal Publishers, 1974).

5. It must be noted that the contemporary usage of the term *giani* is often simply meant to denote those who lead prayers in a Gurudwara or Sikh place of worship. However, Sikhs were traditionally referred to as the circle of *gianis*, that is as knowledgeable and learned persons who had acquired the knowledge of the Creator and creation through a sustained study of the scriptures under the guidance of a spiritual teacher. As Wazir Singh puts it, "Gianis among the Sikh community had a tradition of interpreting the Guru-Granth compositions to the people, of leading a disciplined life that influenced others, and devoting themselves to study, often by way of avocation" (Wazir Singh, *Sikhism: Philosophy and Culture* [New Delhi, National Book Shop, 1999], 17).

6. Nirbahi Singh, *Philosophy of Sikhism: Reality and its Manifestations* (New Delhi: Atlantic Publishers, 1990), 178.

7. Avtar Singh 1996, op cit, 87.

8. Jasbir Singh Ahluwalia, "Inter-religious Relations Today." In *Interfaith Dialogue: Different Perspectives*, edited by Dharam Singh (Patiala: Punjabi University, 2002), 33.

9. From the prayer *Swaiye*, one of the five daily prayers that Sikhs recite, composed by Guru Gobind Singh Ji.

10. I am indebted to Bhai Sahib Mohinder Singh for his clear exposition of this threefold motto.

11. Wazir Singh 1999, op. cit., 36.

12. Wazir Singh 1999, op cit, 38.

13. Dasam Granth, Akal Ustat, 85.

FOUR
A Buddhist Perspective

Sallie B. King

WHAT IS WISDOM?

Wisdom in Buddhism is two kinds of things. First, it is experiential knowledge—as opposed to theoretical or intellectual knowledge—of the Dharma ("Dhamma" in the Pali spelling). The Dharma in Buddhism is Truth and Reality, and also the teachings of the Buddha, which are teachings on Truth and Reality. Second, it is a certain kind of character: negatively, it is freedom from craving, aversion and delusion; positively, it is selflessness, compassion, loving-kindness, deep non-violence and spontaneous morality.

These two aspects of wisdom are two aspects of the same thing, because what we know makes us who we are. As we grow in our experiential understanding of the nature of things, we grow in selflessness, compassion, and related virtues. As we learn more, we change in the profoundest possible way, in our very being.

Wisdom is experiential and non-verbal; it cannot be fully conveyed in words, even the words of the Buddha. The Buddha's teachings are guides to help one find experiential wisdom for oneself, as is taught in the text, the "Simile of the Raft."

In the following passage,[1] the Buddha says that his teachings—the Dhamma—are like a raft. They are a tool, a means to the end of experientially realizing wisdom (the other shore). He says that this tool must be actively used, but not clung to. Moreover, one should not confuse what is a means and what is the true end.

[The Buddha speaks first.]

> "Bhikkhus [monks], I shall show you how the Dhamma is similar to a raft, being for the purpose of crossing over, not for the purpose of grasping. Listen and attend closely to what I shall say . . .
>
> "Bhikkhus, suppose a man in the course of a journey saw a great expanse of water, whose near shore was dangerous and fearful and whose further shore was safe and free from fear, but there was no ferryboat or bridge going to the far shore. Then he thought: 'There is this great expanse of water . . . but there is no ferryboat or bridge going to the far shore. Suppose I collect grass, twigs, branches, and leaves and bind them together into a raft, and supported by the raft and making an effort with my hands and feet, I got safely across to the far shore.' And then the man collected grass, twigs, branches, and leaves and bound them together into a raft, and supported by the raft and making an effort with his hands and feet, he got safely across to the far shore. Then, when he had got across and had arrived at the far shore, he might think thus: 'This raft has been very helpful to me . . . Suppose I were to hoist it on my head or load it on my shoulder, and then go wherever I want.' Now, bhikkhus, what do you think? By doing so, would that man be doing what should be done with that raft?"
>
> "No, venerable sir."
>
> "By doing what would that man be doing what should be done with that raft? Here, bhikkhus, when that man got across and had arrived at the far shore, he might think thus: 'This raft has been very helpful to me, since supported by it and making an effort with my hands and feet, I got safely across to the far shore. Suppose I were to haul it onto the dry land or set it adrift in the water, and then go wherever I want.' Now, bhikkhus, it is by so doing that that man would be doing what should be done with that raft. So I have shown you how the Dhamma is similar to a raft, being for the purpose of crossing over, not for the purpose of grasping."

WHY SHARE?

The Buddha was primarily a teacher of wisdom. A famous story recounts how he decided to teach. According to the traditional life of the Buddha, after the Buddha experienced enlightenment, full experiential knowledge of Truth, he spent some time simply enjoying the bliss of enlightenment. He then considered whether he should teach, sharing the wisdom he had discovered. At first he hesitated, because he knew that the wisdom he had realized was subtle and difficult to understand, whereas humans generally were too wrapped in their delusions and attached to their pleasures to comprehend it. Then the god Brahma Sahampati begged the Buddha to teach, pointing out that at least some could understand him and benefit from his teachings. The Buddha surveyed humankind and, seeing that there were those who would benefit from his teachings, decided to teach out of compassion for the sufferings of sentient beings (beings with awareness, that is, humans, animals and all beings that are reborn again and again in samsara). Compassion for those who suffer, then, is the motivation for sharing wisdom in Buddhism, in the sense of transmitting the Dharma.

But sharing wisdom is a two-way street; there is sharing with others what one has realized and there is receiving from others what they have realized. Contemporary Buddhists recognize at least two important reasons for sharing wisdom in this sense. The first is that it is seen as an essential part of peacemaking, of which two examples follow. In Sri Lanka, where ethnic and religious tensions between Sinhalese Buddhists and Tamil Hindus were one of the roots of that country's recent civil war, the Buddhist organization Sarvodaya Shramadana has worked for five decades to eliminate poverty and, more recently, to make peace. The development work in each village begins with a "family gathering" where villagers decide on a project to pursue. At those gatherings, all the groups present prayers and songs; whichever group is in the minority is given the honor of going first, and all listen respectfully. This kind of relationship became the foundation for Sarvodaya's peacemaking efforts. Since ethnic and religious differences were foundational to the war, it was critical for Sarvodaya's peacemaking efforts that cordial relations with all the ethnic groups and religions already be in place; respectful hearing of each others' religions has been an essential part of those cordial relations. Here the sharing of religious wisdom is at work on two levels at once: the wisdom directly shared in the prayers and songs at the family gatherings (a kind of life wisdom), and the act of wisdom demonstrated in the act of sharing itself.

A second example can be seen in the work of American Zen master, Bernie Glassman. One of his projects has been to take groups to Auschwitz on retreat. Those retreats are made up of Jews, Christians, Buddhists, Muslims, children of Nazis, survivors of the camps, children of survivors, children of German soldiers, and concerned people with no direct link to Auschwitz. They spend five days together, chanting the names of the dead, conducting religious services and rituals from the different religions present, and telling their individual stories. Glassman reports that it is out of hearing each other's stories and bearing witness to their differences that a kind of healing takes place. As Glassman says, Hitler tried to stamp out differences; it is through honoring differences that healing occurs.

A second reason for sharing wisdom that some Buddhists acknowledge today is that they learn spiritually from other religions. Again, we may consider two examples. Taiwanese Buddhist nun Venerable Cheng Yen, founder of the huge Buddhist charity movement Tzu Chi, had developed abundant compassion as a Buddhist, but it took something more for her to begin her charity work. She encountered Catholic nuns who challenged her, saying that there were many Catholic hospitals, schools and charitable enterprises but no Buddhist ones; "what do Buddhists ever contribute to society?" she was asked. After this encounter, Ven. Cheng Yen reflected that, in the past, Buddhists haven't known how to implement the Buddha's teachings of wisdom and compassion in society. This showed her the way forward and she began the Tzu Chi organization, which gives free medical care to anyone who asks for it and in which millions of people are volunteers.

A second example is, again, American Zen master Bernie Glassman. Glassman tells a story from his early days as a teacher, when he was listening to a group of Catholic nuns speak of their meditation experience and what it means for their relationship with God. Glassman, who, as a Buddhist, does not believe in God, wondered to himself with dismay how they could still believe in God after meditating for so long. He immediately saw his own arrogance in those thoughts and realized that he himself didn't know as much as he thought he knew, especially since his spiritual practice is based on inquiry and openness. He ultimately learned that there is no conflict between meditation and belief in God. He now is happy when his Zen students go to a local Sufi center for zikr (Sufi prayer—which, of course, involves God), in addition to their Zen Buddhist practice.

HOW DO WE SHARE?

Context

Although religions had clear identities in the Asian countries where Buddhism found itself in pre-modern times, they did not strictly separate themselves from each other. There was always a tendency toward lots of give and take among religions. For example, Thailand was animistic before Buddhism arrived. When Buddhism came to the country, virtually all Thais became Buddhists (except some people in remote areas), but they did not give up animism. Today you will see the "spirit houses" that house the animistic spirits everywhere in Thailand, including on Buddhist temple grounds.

In China, Buddhism encountered another culture every bit as sophisticated as its native India, with highly developed religions in Confucianism and Taoism; in this case, relations were more complex. There was a great deal of competition and debate among the three great religious traditions, Buddhism, Confucianism, and Taoism, and a great deal of absorption of ideas from each other. Zen Buddhism, which came into being as Indian Buddhism adjusted to Chinese culture, is the product of Buddhism absorbing a great deal of Taoist wisdom. Neo-Confucianism absorbed a great deal from Buddhism. There was also a strong tendency, throughout East Asia, for people to simultaneously "be" more than one religion. In China, for example, there was the syncretistic "Three Religions" (Buddhism, Confucianism, Taoism), which for centuries was the common faith of all. In Japan, most traditional people "were" both Shinto and Buddhist—actually, people didn't think in these terms; they just practiced both religions, which they felt to be the Japanese ethos. These religions were often seen as complementary, rather than competing, i.e., dealing with different aspects of spirituality.

Imparting

As a teacher, the Buddha taught with great openness. He walked throughout his region of India from village to village, speaking with whoever wanted to hear him. Unlike some other teachers in his time, the Buddha taught "with an open hand," that is, without holding anything back from anyone. He taught people of both genders and all social classes and castes. If they wanted to hear what he had to say, he would share his wisdom. If they did not want to hear, he would go mildly on his way. The Buddha was happy to participate in discussions and debates on the basis of truth, as he said, and frequently did. Later Buddhists have done the same over the centuries.

As a universal religion (that is, a religion that believes its message is universal, appropriate for everyone), Buddhism has always welcomed converts. But the Buddha himself would not push hard for conversion. He simply would present the teaching, and people responded to it however they did. In fact, the Buddha is on record as asking a man named Upali who wanted to convert to Buddhism from Jainism to think it over first and consider carefully before converting, because the man was such a prominent Jain. When Upali remained adamant about converting, the Buddha accepted him as a convert but told him that he must continue to support his former religion with donations (which was how such groups survived).

Though Buddhism is spreading rapidly in the West today, Buddhist teachers continue to follow the Buddha's example, simply presenting the teaching openly and letting people respond however they will. The goal is typically not to get people to convert to Buddhism as such, but to spread the Dharma, which means to encourage people to seek wisdom and to cultivate compassion and loving-kindness. Some prominent teachers, such as His Holiness the Dalai Lama and Thich Nhat Hanh, often discourage people from converting to Buddhism, saying the religions that people were born in are perfectly good forms of religious practice. Of course, some people in the West do convert to Buddhism and they are welcome, but many, many more Westerners continue to understand themselves to "be" Jewish or Christian but, perhaps, do Buddhist meditation or read Buddhist books, taking these ideas and practices into their lives and their worldview. In some cases, they say that this brings greater depth, or new life, to their Judaism or Christianity.

Receiving

As discussed above, a great deal of giving and taking among religions was the norm in countries where Buddhism found itself. Of course, it is considerably rarer for Buddhists who were literate and erudite enough to be writing and sufficiently esteemed for those writings to be preserved, to say in writing what they learned from non-Buddhists. However, examples can be found.

In China, while there was a great deal of mutual esteem and two-way sharing between Buddhists and Taoists (at least when they weren't competing for imperial patronage), relations between Buddhists and Confucianists often tended to be less cordial, as the two religions initially had little in common. However, even here there are examples of Buddhist willingness to acknowledge Confucian wisdom. Buddhist monk Seng Chao (384–414) was a leading thinker during the period in which Chinese Buddhists interpreted Buddhism in Taoist terms. He was strongly influenced by Taoism and occasionally also had a good word to say about Confucianism, quoting both the Taoist philosopher Chuang Tzu and Confucius in his writings. In the Republican period in China, the standard curriculum in Buddhist seminaries required mastery of the Confucian classics (the Four Books and the Five Classics). When the eminent monk Hsu-yun visited Ch'u-fu in 1900 he paid his respects at the temple and tomb of Confucius.[2]

In Japan, the great Japanese Zen master, Hakuin Ekaku, (1686–1786) was a lifelong devotee of the Shinto deity Tenjin (the deified Sugawara no Michizane, the god of learning) and, throughout his life, rose at 2:00 a.m. every morning to worship him.[3] Soto Zen monk Ryokan (1758–1831), though famed for his poetry and calligraphy, lived a life of intentional poverty and simplicity and practiced religion as the common Japanese people practiced it. He was famously nonsectarian and served for a time as caretaker of a Shinto shrine.[4] Both of these men were major figures, two of the most famous Japanese Zen monks of all time. Hakuin was a major reviver of Rinzai Zen and is often called the "father of modern Zen." Ryokan is intensely beloved and is often said to represent the "essence" of traditional Japan.

In modern times, Buddhists more often express the value they have found in non-Buddhist teachings. Japanese Buddhist philosopher Masao Abe initiated and actively pursued dialogue with Christians from 1963 until his death in 2006. In 1989, he published a paper titled, "The Impact of Dialogue with Christianity on My Self-Understanding as a Buddhist." In it, he lists three areas in which dialogue with Christianity had altered his philosophical thinking.

First, he said, Christian inability to understand the core Buddhist concept of sunyata, translated into English as "emptiness," led him to clarify his own thinking on sunyata and emphasize the positive and soteriological meanings of sunyata, its dynamic function and openness. Second, in the area of ethics, he realized that Buddhism lacked a concept of justice. He suggested ways to bring out Buddhist ideas that express the idea of fairness, though he rejected connotations of judgmentalism and punishment associated with the Western concept of justice. Finally, he came to recognize that, due to its emphasis on a timeless wisdom, Buddhism's view of history is very weak, and he suggested that the idea of compassion, with which wisdom is paired in Buddhism, could be the foundation of seeing action within time as something of value.[5]

More typical of Buddhist learning from non-Buddhist religion in the modern world has been Buddhist learning about putting wisdom and compassion into concrete action in the world. Some of this we have already seen above, for example, in the Tzu Chi movement. The movement called "Engaged Buddhism," of which Tzu Chi is a part, exhibits considerable learning from other religions. This is a contemporary movement that aims to apply Buddhist principles in engagement with the social, political and economic issues of their societies. The greatest single influence on this group is Mahatma Gandhi. Sarvodaya Shramadana, discussed above, originated when its founder, Dr. A. T. Ariyaratne, studied in person with Gandhi's successor, Vinoba Bhave. The name, "Sarvodaya," is itself taken from the Gandhian movement, where it meant "the welfare of all"; Ariyaratne has re-interpreted it as meaning "the awakening of all." Gandhi is also important to His Holiness, the Dalai Lama, who has written of the great example that Gandhi is for him.

Process—Skillful Means and Advice

The experiential nature of wisdom in Buddhism means that it cannot be shared directly; it must be discovered experientially by each person. By its very nature, this wisdom transcends all words and images, anything that we might say or think of it. But what can be shared is the "finger pointing at the moon." The moon here represents the wisdom we are trying to realize. All of the Buddha's teachings, and the teachings of subsequent teachers, are fingers pointing at the moon. One consequence of this view is that one should not be attached to one's views since, no matter what they are, they can never be more than the finger pointing at the moon. One should take them seriously enough to be guided by them, and yet one must hold them lightly and be prepared to adjust or drop them as one grows in experiential understanding.

Because wisdom cannot be stated adequately, the Buddha made a point of adjusting his teachings in relation to the capacity of his audience to understand him. Thus flexibility in the forms of expressing and communicating Buddhism became a principle that in the Mahayana schools is called "skillful means": one should adjust the form of the teaching as appropriate in order to communicate effectively. This principle greatly aided Buddhism as it spread from India into other countries, as it allowed it to adjust itself to different cultures.

In modern times, the idea of skillful means has been restated by Vietnamese monk Thich Nhat Hanh. Thich Nhat Hanh's teaching has always stressed the importance of remembering that the forms in which the Dharma can be expressed must be flexible, since they are not the essential part (the Dharma is). Following are three precepts of the Order of Interbeing, created by Thich Nhat Hanh.[6]

> *First*: Do not be idolatrous about or bound to any doctrine, theory, or ideology, even Buddhist ones. All systems of thought are guiding means; they are not absolute truth.
>
> *Second*: Do not think that the knowledge you presently possess is changeless, absolute truth. Avoid being narrow-minded and bound to present views. Learn and practice non-attachment from views in order to be open to receive others' viewpoints. Truth is found in life and not merely in conceptual knowledge. Be ready to learn throughout your entire life and to observe reality in yourself and in the world at all times.
>
> *Third*: Do not force others, including children, by any means whatsoever, to adopt your views, whether by authority, threat, money, propaganda, or even education. However, through compassionate dialogue, help others renounce fanaticism and narrowness.[7]

These precepts echo the Parable of the Raft in sharply distinguishing between wisdom, or truth, and the means for realizing truth, between the pointing finger and the moon. Nhat Hanh points out that, because reality changes from moment to moment, we need to remain alert to what is happening in the present, in order to know what is true right now. Nhat Hanh cites the traditional saying that the Buddha opened "10,000 Dharma doors" (that is, he taught the Dharma in 10,000 ways), but says that we need to open even more!

Thai lay leader Sulak Sivaraksa differentiates between "big B" Buddhism and "little b" buddhism. The former is institutionalized Buddhism, which may be benign or may become aligned with potentially negative forces such as nationalism. "Little b" buddhism is Buddhist values at their best—such values as selflessness, generosity and compassion. This does not imply that Buddhism "owns" these values in a way that other religions do not; to the contrary, Sulak and other leaders often emphasize that these values can be found in all the major religions. The important thing to share, they say, is the selflessness, generosity and compassion, and ways for developing them, not the "big B" Buddhism.

RESPONSIBLE SHARING

In ancient India, where Buddhism originated, many religious views peacefully co-existed side-by-side; teachings, discussions, and debates about religion were common. With many different teachings being shared by wandering teachers, ancient India could be a challenging place to decide what one's religious views were! The Buddha gave some famous advice to the inhabitants of a village called Kalama about how to handle this situation.[8]

> [Villagers from Kalama in Kesaputta speak first; the Buddha replies.]
> "Venerable sir, some ascetics and brahmins who come to Kesaputta explain and elucidate their own doctrines, but disparage, debunk revile, and vilify the doctrines of others. But then some other ascetics and brahmins come to Kesaputta, and they too explain and elucidate their own doctrines, but disparage, debunk, revile, and vilify the doctrines of the others. For us, venerable sir, there is perplexity and doubt as to which of these good ascetics speak truth and which speak falsehood."
>
> "It is fitting for you to be perplexed, O Kalamas, it is fitting for you to be in doubt. Doubt has arisen in you about a perplexing matter. Come, Kalamas. Do not go by oral tradition, by lineage of teaching, by hearsay, by a collection of texts, by logic, by inferential reasoning, by reasoned cogitation, by the acceptance of a view after pondering it, by the seeming competence of a speaker, or because you think, 'The ascetic is our teacher.' But when you know for yourselves, 'These things are unwholesome; these things are blamable; these things are censured by the wise; these things, if undertaken and practiced, lead to harm and suffering,' then you should abandon them . . . [And] when you know for yourselves, 'These things are wholesome; these things are blameless; these things are praised by the wise; these things, if undertaken and practiced, lead to welfare and happiness,' then you should engage in them."

The Buddha tells the inhabitants of Kalama that they should not accept any teaching on the basis of authority, tradition, the fact that it is given in a sacred text, or even logic, but only on the basis of what they know for certain for themselves in their own experience. He suggests a pragmatic test for what to believe: if something causes pain and suffering, he said, give it up; if it is wholesome and frees one from suffering, practice it.

The Buddha found certain views to be particularly pernicious, and he warned his followers about them. These are: nihilistic materialism (the view that only material things exist and that after death there is nothing; which means there is no karma, and both human relations and religious action are meaningless), amorality (there are no consequences for good or bad deeds), non-causality (there is no real relation between cause and effect), and fatalism (no matter what you do, things turn out the same).[9]

The effect of each of these views is to make following a religious life, as the Buddha understood it, pointless.

The wanderer Sandaka asks a question and Venerable Ananda, a monk close to the Buddha, replies:[10]

> "Master Ananda, what are those four ways that negate the living of the holy life that have been declared by the Blessed One [the Buddha] . . . wherein a wise man certainly would not live the holy life, or if he should live it, would not attain the true way, the Dhamma that is wholesome?"
>
> "Here, Sandaka, some teacher holds such a doctrine and view as this: [1] 'There is nothing given, nothing offered, nothing sacrificed; no fruit or result of good and bad actions; no this world, no other world . . . A person consists of the four great elements . . . Fools and the wise are alike cut off and annihilated with the dissolution of the body; after death they do not exist.' [2] 'If one were to go along the south bank of the Ganges slaughtering, mutilating . . . and torturing . . . because of this there would be no evil and no outcome of evil. If one were to go along the north bank of the Ganges giving gifts . . . and making offerings . . . because of this there would be no merit and no outcome of merit.' [3] 'There is no cause or condition for the defilement of beings . . . there is no cause or condition for the purification of beings . . . All beings, all living things, all creatures . . . are without mastery, power, and energy, moulded by destiny, circumstance, and nature . . .' [4] '. . . The round of rebirths is limited, there is no shortening or extending it, no increasing or decreasing it. Just as a ball of string when thrown goes as far as the string unwinds, so too, by running and wandering through the round of rebirths, fools and the wise both will make an end of suffering.'"
>
> "These, Sandaka, are the four ways that negate the living of the holy life that have been declared by the Blessed One [the Buddha] . . . wherein a wise man certainly would not live the holy life, or if he should live it, would not attain the true way, the Dhamma that is wholesome."

According to the Buddha, these four views are of no possible spiritual value, because they make meaningless any spiritual effort. Making a spiritual effort is indispensable and it would be very difficult for Buddhists to make common cause with any view that made the religious life pointless. Because Truth is fundamentally ineffable, there is no strong reason not to make common cause with other religions, even if they see things somewhat differently, as long as living a good life, striving to improve oneself, and the like are considered worthwhile. However, Buddhists tend to see religions that are forcefully dogmatic or arrogantly convinced of their own superiority as quite wrong-headed and offensive.

In the contemporary world, Buddhists have new kinds of concerns. With globalization and Westernization hitting Buddhist Asia hard, many thoughtful Buddhists are concerned about their cultures and religions being overwhelmed by the seductive appeal of Western culture, with its combination of wealth and power and the allure of its television programs, movies, music, and an affluent, hedonistic lifestyle that seems to promise a life of greater pleasure and ease. The Thai lay leader Sulak Sivaraksa has been particularly active in his efforts to preserve traditional Thai culture from Westernization, while at the same time finding ways to reform and modernize Buddhism to make it more responsive to contemporary global conditions and needs.

Does Globalization Threaten Religions?

Some traditional Buddhists find distasteful the commodification of Buddhism, with Zen clocks and Tibetan wall calendars seeming to package and sell Buddhism in the West, though some traditional Buddhists find new avenues of livelihood in selling such products and may well see such work as Right Livelihood (a part of Buddhist practice for the layperson). On the other hand, globalization has also opened important new doors for Buddhists—Tibetan Buddhists, in particular, who had for centuries kept many teachings hidden, have in recent decades openly publicized some formerly hidden teachings for fear that they might be lost due to the occupation of the Tibetan homeland by the Chinese and the latter's active suppression of Tibetan Buddhism.

Another factor limiting some Buddhists' sharing of wisdom in the modern world is the concern of dalit Buddhists—persons formerly belonging to the "scheduled" castes, or so-called "untouchables"—who converted from Hinduism to Buddhism in an effort to shed their Hindu identities and the abysmally low social class that was an integral part of that identity. To these "new" Buddhists, it is important that they free themselves entirely of their Hindu habits and thought patterns. Their Buddhist identity is fragile and they feel a need for a clean break from Hinduism. When they convert to Buddhism, they take a vow neither to worship Hindu gods, nor to engage in Hindu practices, and they formally renounce Hinduism. They may be quite hostile toward Hinduism and are in no way open to the idea of sharing wisdom with Hindus. The fact that some Hindu nationalists consider the dalit Buddhists to be just another sect of Hinduism reinforces the dalits' sense of needing to insist upon their separation and difference from Hinduism.

SPECIFIC WISDOMS

To Offer

Buddhism at its best is able to differentiate between the means of realizing wisdom and wisdom itself, the raft and the other shore, as expressed in the Simile of the Raft. In this way, it is able to see itself as a path, a means of accessing wisdom, not as identical with that wisdom or as having exclusive possession of it. Of course, not all Buddhists think this way, but it is a teaching of the Buddha nonetheless. This view opens the door to a self-understanding and a modesty that seem very appropriate in a world of many religions, none of which can prove their claims to the satisfaction of the others!

Because it sees itself as a path to the realization of wisdom, Buddhism has developed many concrete practices that people can use to develop their spiritual lives, and Buddhists are happy to share them with non-Buddhists. Many of these—such as practices to develop inner peace, compassion or loving-kindness—are not particularly Buddhist per se, and can be used by people of any religion, or of none. Mindfulness meditation practices stripped of all their Buddhist trappings are used in hospitals today to help people reduce their stress and handle chronic pain. From a Buddhist point of view, anything that helps to reduce suffering is good.

To Receive

There is something of a consensus among contemporary Buddhists who participate in global discussions about religion that Buddhism has the most to learn from other religions in the area of learning how to put their compassion and loving-kindness into practice in concrete action in the world. This process involves developing forms of action, but it may also require a rethinking of the status and value of things such as human history and human relationships. Many important new forms of Buddhist social action were developed in the twentieth century, but this process has farther to go. Also, partly as a result of its encounters with other religions and cultures, Buddhists are just beginning to re-examine and amend the status of women in Buddhist institutions, teachings and cultures; this process has much farther to go.

FORGIVENESS AND LOVE

Buddhism counts wisdom and compassion as the two defining marks of a Buddha and, in fact, sees wisdom and compassion as two sides of a single coin, because wisdom is the realization that we are not fundamentally separate from each other. Anger is considered an unskillful and harmful response, no matter the provocation.

> Following is the classical teaching of the Buddha:[11]
> 'He reviled me! He struck me!
> He defeated me! He robbed me!'
> They who gird themselves up with this,
> For them enmity is not quelled.

'He reviled me! He struck me!
He defeated me! He robbed me!'
They who do not gird themselves up with this,
For them is enmity quelled.
Not by enmity are enmities quelled, whatever the occasion here.
By the absence of enmity are they quelled.
This is an ancient truth.

This text, taken from the *Dhammapada*, makes several important points. (1) How you react to wrongs done to you is your own responsibility. One harms oneself by maintaining feelings of anger and resentment for two reasons. First, such feelings are painful; if one prolongs them, one is causing oneself unnecessary pain. Second, feelings of anger will cause one to behave unskillfully, inviting future suffering toward oneself. (2) Enmity or conflict cannot be overcome by aggressive acts. Responding to violence with violence simply continues a cycle of violence. Enmity or conflict can only be overcome by self-controlled and restrained behavior that rises above reacting out of anger and rationally looks for the best response.

In Buddhist practice, one makes an effort to intentionally cultivate the states of being or character traits that the tradition holds as ideals. One set of practices cultivates a whole family of ideals related to wisdom and love called the "Four Immeasurables": loving-kindness, defined as wishing others well (this term is sometimes translated as "love" in English); compassion, or being concerned about the suffering of others; sympathetic joy or joy experienced in response to others doing well; and equanimity or imperturbability.

> First of all loving-kindness should again and again be developed for oneself, "May I be happy, free from ill," or, "May I be free from enmity, free from injury, free from disturbance, and may I preserve myself at ease!" Developing the wish, "May I be well," and taking himself as a witness, the disciple produces then the wish that other beings also should have well-being and ease, i.e., "As I want to be happy, am averse to suffering, want to live and do not want to die, so also other beings." In order that he may take himself as a witness, he must first of all radiate loving-kindness on to himself. Immediately after that . . . he should think of his dear, pleasant, respected teacher or preceptor, or of someone who is like him, as well as of his generosity, his friendly words, etc., which make him so dear and pleasant, and of his moral virtue, learning, etc., which make him so respected. And the disciple should develop loving-kindness for him, in this manner: "May this good man be free from ill," and so on. . . . But the monk who is not content with just that . . . should immediately after that develop loving-kindness for a very dear person, then for an indifferent person, then for an enemy. . . . If, while he directs his mind on to the enemy, aversion arises in him on remembering the offences that enemy has committed, he should again and again accomplish an attitude of loving-kindness

> toward the first three kinds of person. Then, emerging from that, he should dispel the aversion by again and again feeling loving-kindness toward that last person (i.e., the enemy) . . .
>
> Then, as he feels loving-kindness again and again, he should achieve an even mind toward the four persons—i.e., himself, a dear person, an indifferent person, a foe—and bring about the abolition of the barriers between them.[12]

The states described in this text are developed gradually, starting by cultivating the particular state of being for a particular person to whom it is relatively easy to apply that posture, working through progressively more challenging individuals until one reaches the most difficult one. For example, you begin cultivating loving-kindness by focusing upon yourself, then move to someone who has done something kind for you; then to a very dear person, such as a beloved family member; then to an acquaintance toward whom one feels neutral; and, finally, to an enemy, or someone who has harmed you. The objective is to cultivate loving-kindness for each of these particular people until the loving-kindness that one feels toward each one of them is identical.

Buddhism maintains high ideals of love and compassion, but it is also practical in developing concrete behaviors to help one to be able to be the kind of person who can love his or her enemy. Wisdom helps in this, by helping us to understand that people do harmful or "unskillful" things for reasons. As His Holiness, the Dalai Lama, often points out, all people are alike in wanting to be happy, but some people are very unskillful in the things that they do to try to gain that state. Moreover, we live in a karmic world, that is, one in which events occur due to the confluence of multiple causes and conditions. Some people have been raised in ignorance or fear or terrible need. Some have been taught from childhood to hate; others have experienced terrible tragedy or loss and have become embittered. Such people may find happiness in killing, having their revenge upon those who killed a loved one. When one understands the reasons, however twisted, behind a hateful action, one sees it very differently and reacts accordingly. This is one aspect of karma; another is that one's own actions are sowing seeds that will construct one's own future experiences. If I act in a loving way, I construct a pleasant future for myself; if I act hatefully, I construct future suffering for myself. Therefore, even if someone does something hateful to oneself, one should not react in a hateful way, or one will only cause oneself further harm. One should practice in order to gain self-mastery.

Then, if and when something painful does happen to oneself, one's family, or one's community, one will have the self-discipline not to lash out blindly in a way that could make the situation worse and will certainly earn oneself bad karma. Instead, if one has self-control, one can examine the situation composedly and choose the best response under those particular circumstances. This is the idea behind the first two stanzas from the *Dhammapada* quoted above (on page 56–57). The last stanza states that the law of karma is a law of the universe, according to which hateful acts only produce more hateful acts in response. Whether an individual or a nation, if one strikes another, the one who has been hit will respond accordingly.

The only possible way out of this situation is for an individual or a group to have the wisdom and self-discipline to rise above such angry retaliation and offer an alternative. Such peacemakers (e.g., Mahatma Gandhi, Yitzhak Rabin, and Martin Luther King Jr.) are often killed because there are still many "karmic seeds" of hatred that have been sown and are in the process of coming to fruition when such pioneers step forward. But they plant seeds of peace that make it easier for the next one who comes along, and the next.

How the teachings of the *Dhammapada* guide contemporary Buddhist role-models is seen in the activities of Samdech Preah Maha Ghosananda at the end of the rule of the Khmer Rouge.

From 1975 to 1979, the communist Khmer Rouge controlled Cambodia. Their rule resulted in somewhere between one and three million dead (out of a population of approximately 7.5 million in 1975) from execution, torture, starvation, displacement and forced labor. Particularly targeted were Buddhist monks, who were almost entirely wiped out, and anyone who seemed to be an intellectual. The cities were emptied out and people forced to live in the countryside. Buddhist temples were used for torture and the storage of weapons.

When the Khmer Rouge era ended, the response of the Cambodian Buddhist leadership, particularly Samdech Preah Maha Ghosananda, was to focus on the healing of the wounds of the people and the reconciliation of the four mutually-hostile camps within Cambodia which were fully capable of continuing armed hostilities.

To help with the healing of the people's wounds, Maha Ghosananda entered the refugee camps reciting the *Metta Sutta* and verse 5 of the *Dhammapada* (quoted above) as people wept. He urged people to let go of the past and move forward in their lives. The Cambodian people generally bore in mind the teachings of karma and forewent seeking revenge as they saw this as only prolonging the cycle of suffering, and they did not want themselves, or their children, to suffer any further. Maha Ghosananda led the Dhammayietra movement which accompanied refugees home, visited isolated villages still threatened by violence, and supported the voting that made the institution of a new government possible.

He reflected on the way in which he was able to use Buddhist wisdom to bring about reconciliation:

> In 1981 . . . we held a Buddhist ceremony for peace. At the end of the ceremony, a Khmer Rouge leader came up to me, very cautiously, and

asked if I would come to Thailand to build a temple at the border. I said that I would.

"Oh!" thought many people, "he is talking to the enemy. He is helping the enemy! How can he do that?" I reminded them that love embraces all beings, whether they are noble-minded or low-minded, good or evil.

Both the noble and the good are embraced because loving kindness flows to them spontaneously. The unwholesome-minded must be included because they are the ones who need loving kindness the most. In many of them, the seed of goodness may have died because warmth was lacking for its growth. It perished from coldness in a world without compassion. . . .

I do not question that loving one's oppressors—Cambodians loving the Khmer Rouge—may be the most difficult attitude to achieve. But it is a law of the universe that retaliation, hatred, and revenge only continue the cycle and never stop it. Reconciliation does not mean that we surrender rights and conditions, but rather that we use love in all of our negotiations.[13]

NOTES

1. From the Buddha: The Simile of the Raft (*Majjhima Nikaya*, Sutta 22 *Alagaddupama Sutta*).

2. Holmes Welch, *The Practice of Chinese Buddhism 1900–1950* (Cambridge, MA: Harvard University Press, 1967), 400–1.

3. John Stevens, *Three Zen Masters: Ikkyu, Hakuin, and Ryokan* (Tokyo: Kodansha International, 1993), 60.

4. Ryuichi Abe and Peter Haskel, translators and editors, *Great Fool: Zen Master Ryokan—Poems, Letters, and Other Writings* (Honolulu: University of Hawaii Press, 1996), 21.

5. Masao Abe, "The Impact of Dialogue with Christianity on My Self-Understanding as a Buddhist," *Buddhist-Christian Studies* 9 (1989): 62–70.

6. Thich Nhat Hanh, *Being Peace* (Berkeley, CA: Parallax Press, 1987), 89, 90, 91.

7. Thich Nhat Hanh urges Buddhists not to be attached to Buddhist teachings. Notice how this passage continues ideas from the Simile of the Raft passage.

8. From the Buddha: Advice to the Kalamas (*Anguttara Nikaya* 3:65).

9. *Majjhima Nikaya*, Sutta, 76 (*Sandaka Sutta*). *The Middle Length Discourses of the Buddha: A New Translation of the Majjhima Nikaya*, trans. by Bhikkhu Nanamoli and Bhikkhu Bodhi (Boston: Wisdom Publications, 1995), 619–23.

10. Four ways that negate the living of the holy life, taught by the Venerable Ananda on behalf of the Buddha. (*Majjhima Nikaya, Sutta, 76, Sandaka Sutta*).

11. *Dhammapada*, verses 3–5. Translated by John Ross Carter and Mahinda Palihawadana (Oxford: Oxford University Press, 1987).

12. *Visuddhimagga* of Buddhaghosa, translated by Edward Conze in *Buddhist Meditation* (New York: Harper and Row, 1956). (The present author has substituted the translation "loving-kindness" for "friendliness" in the original).

13. From Maha Ghosananda, *Step By Step* (Berkeley, CA: Parallax Press, 1992).

FIVE
A Muslim Perspective

Timothy J. Gianotti

WHAT IS WISDOM?

How does the Islamic tradition conceive of wisdom? Are there different kinds or modalities of wisdom? Is it possible to share any or all of this wisdom with others? Why would or should Muslims be interested in doing this? How should they? These questions, like all questions in the realm of Islamic spirituality, practice, and religious thought, lead to a living encounter between the historical, political, and even existential forces that shape us, on the one hand, and an ancient, Arabic text, on the other, a "book" that is believed to be timeless in its relevance and authority for life. This chapter will seek to be conscious of both sides of this encounter as it explores these questions and their implications for Muslims and their religious cousins and neighbors.

Turning then first to the Qur'ān, the "book" believed to be the collected recitations revealed by God to the Prophet Muhammad through the mediation of the Angel Gabriel some 1400 years ago, the text that serves as the fountainhead for all traditional Islamic knowledge and guidance, we begin.

> And do not take the signs of God in a frivolous spirit; and remember the blessings with which God has graced you and all that He has revealed to you of the Book and the wisdom in order to instruct and admonish you thereby; and be vigilantly conscious of God and know that God knows everything.
>
> *al-Qur'ān, sūra(t) al-baqara* / the cow (2): 231[1]

In the Arabic of the Qur'ān, Wisdom (*ḥikmah*) is expressed by the trilateral root Ḥ + K + M (ح + ك + م), a three letter equation that carries a range of meanings, from a kind of supra-sensible and super-rational knowledge and understanding to more pragmatic notions of discernment, judgment, governance, and right living. As a religious concept, or collection of interrelated concepts, Wisdom cannot be conceived apart from God and revelation (indeed, Wisdom is rarely mentioned in the Qur'ān apart from revelation,[2] and the Qur'ān itself is described as the "Wise Book"[3]). These essential associations bring Wisdom into close contact with other terms that relate to the revelation, terms such as knowledge,[4] guidance, discernment, and light.

Wisdom, then, in the Islamic spiritual traditions, is

> The most sublime mode of knowledge, and the sublimity of knowledge is proportioned to the sublimity of its object, and there is none more sublime than God—great and glorious . . . whoever knows God the most high is wise, even if his aptitude be deficient in the other conventional modes of knowledge, or his speech be slow or faltering in expounding them.[5]

Insofar as Wisdom itself is understood to be one of God's attributes or qualities and involves the understanding of Divinity itself, it is connected intimately to the Divine Essence, which is eternally beyond (*akbar*) all natural human understanding. Wisdom, then, like knowledge and the other Divine qualities, cannot ever be naturally "acquired" or "possessed" by a human being. It can be, however, imparted by God upon a person, just as the Qur'ān describes God's bestowal of wisdom upon Lot,[6] Luqmān,[7] David,[8] Jesus,[9] John,[10] and others to whom God wills to give it.[11] In the form of revelation, Wisdom can also be said to be imparted upon whole communities, although the Qur'ān frequently reminds its readers that most people do not recognize the Truth laid before them and turn away.[12] The ones who do recognize it and do not turn away are the elect few, referred to in the Qur'ān by such descriptions as "those who are endowed with insight"[13] (*ūlū 'l-albāb*), "those endowed with knowledge" (*ūlū 'l-'ilm*), and "the well-grounded in knowledge"[14] (*al-rāsikhūna fī'l-'ilm*). These, then, would be the ones who recognize Truth and reshape their lives around the Wisdom bestowed upon them, while others may have the book but no share in the Wisdom it offers. The wise person, then, lives in an altered state of mind, a state in which particulars are considered in the light of universals and everything in this world is perceived in the light of the Hereafter.[15]

> He is the God (Allāh), the Creator, the Maker, the Fashioner. To Him belong the Most Beautiful Names; everything in the heavens and on the earth proclaims His glory, and He is the Mighty, the Wise. (59:24)

From God's perspective, then, the sharing of Wisdom is not a sharing between equals, each having a wisdom to share with the other; rather, it is the sharing between an all-knowing, all-powerful, solitary possessor of Knowledge and Wisdom[16] and a servant who has nothing to offer in return save his or her self. Individually, this one-way "sharing" of the Divine quality or attribute is believed to be possible when the servant struggles to make his or her way out of the trappings of self-delusion (self-importance, independence, pride, judgment, etc.) and shed all his/her ungodly attributes (ultimately even shedding personal will). As the heart gradually empties of these impediments, it is said to grow in its purified desire for true Wisdom and Knowledge and so embody the Qur'anic supplication, "My Lord! Increase me in knowledge!"

The nearer the servant comes, the more God is said to love him or her, and—in the context of that love—the more transformed the servant becomes. Some have called this transformation the "exchanging of attributes" or qualities, and so Wisdom does not come alone as a separate grace or charism but comes rather as part of a larger host of qualities and virtues that come to perfect the soul and restore her to her original and true nature, which the Qur'ān describes as being the "most beautiful" form or constitution ("fī ahsani taqwīm")[17]—which places the restored human being above even the ranks of the angels.[18]

There are many Qur'ānic passages and Prophetic traditions that speak of the love and transformation God bestows upon individuals, including the prophets. In *sūra(t) Tā Hā* (20), we see God speaking directly to the baby Moses,

> I have cast over you [the garment of] love from Me in order that you may be reared under My eye. (20:39)

Here God's love is given to the baby Moses, who is assured of God's protection, care, and guidance as he grows. Nothing of course is required in response to this gift, but that seems to change when the address is directed toward adults. In *sūra(t) āl-'Imrān* / the family of 'Imrān (3), we see the adult Prophet Muhammad addressed with a command to proclaim a different love equation:

> Say: "If you love God, then follow me. God will love you and forgive your sins." For God is Oft-Forgiving, Most Merciful. (3:31)

Here, we see the promise of God's love and forgiveness in response to the individual's love and obedience. The transformative implications of this love are, however, left unaddressed and so wait for another revealed word to be explained.

In one of the sacred traditions (*ahādīth qudsīyah*), the extra-Qur'ānic theopathic sayings through which God is believed to have spoken directly to the people through the Prophet Muhammad, we read

> Whoever shows enmity to someone devoted to Me, I shall be at war with him. My servant does not draw nigh unto Me by anything more beloved to Me than that which I have enjoined upon him [i.e., the religious duties], and My servant continues to draw nigh unto Me by [performing] superogatory acts [of devotion] so that I [come to] love him. And, when I love him, I am his hearing by which he hears, his sight by which he sees, his hand by which he strikes, and his leg by which he walks. Were he to ask Me [for something], surely I would give it to him; were he to ask Me for refuge, surely I would grant it.

Here again we see love and devotion expressed in the form of obedience, and God's promise of love, protection, and transformation in return. Such texts, taken together with the notion of the soul's restoration / perfection in the Divine qualities, seem to suggest a mysterious and intimate identification of the soul with or within God. While traditional Muslim scholars and sages, such as Abū Hāmid al-Ghazālī (d. 1111 CE), have piously maintained that there must always be a formal distinction between Creator and creature and have thus cautioned Muslims to understand that they will only ever be able to acquire something resembling God's attributes (not the Divine attributes as they truly are in relation to the Divine),[19] there is no doubt that the psycho-spiritual process of coming into one's full nature—as a human being—mysteriously involves the taking on of God's qualities: the Merciful, the Wise, the Knowing, the Compassionate, the Clement, the Oft-Forgiving, the Giver of Safety and Sanctuary, the Living, the Powerful, the Forbearing, the Subtle, etc.[20] In this way, the tradition says the heart becomes a polished mirror or cleansed tablet in which the Divine qualities are reflected rather than an independent possessor of the Divine qualities.[21]

To this end, we find a number of Muslim spiritual sages, including al-Ghazālī, citing an unconfirmed tradition in which the Prophet is reported to have coached his companions to "put on the qualities of God Most High." In a more widely accepted tradition, the Prophet is reported to have said, "God has ninety-nine attributes, i.e., one hundred less one; whosoever believes in them and acts accordingly will enter the Garden."[22]

To sum up our findings thus far, then, Wisdom is Qur'ānically understood to be a Divine quality in which humans can share, a knowledge or understanding of Divinity itself that is imparted upon a human being on account of God's love and mercy and in accord with the mystery of God's design and decree. The bestowal of this Divine attribute is understood to be a mind-altering and life altering experience, by which the servant comes to see this mundane world through the lens of eternity. This is what it means to be wise.

KNOWLEDGE AND WISDOM

The Qur'ānic sense of the term seems to connect practical advice for living, on the one hand, and esoteric knowledge, on the other. In both cases it seems to indicate the way we live in relation to knowledge or Truth. In the sūrah devoted to the discourses of the wise prophet Luqmān, we read the advice to avoid associating anyone or anything with God, to be respectful of one's parents, to keep up a life of prayer and patience, and to walk humbly through life.[23] Here Wisdom seems to be the practical extension or application of knowledge—not knowledge in the sense of information or discursive, deliberative knowledge, but God's "knowledge of the unseen [aspects] of the heavens,"[24] a knowledge that is secret, esoteric, and beyond conventional rational processes. This is the knowledge bestowed upon Adam but barred from the angels, the knowledge of "the names" or true essences of things.[25] This is also the knowledge that penetrates into the hidden meanings that underlie the seemingly random and perplexing events of life.

In another passage, making reference to a special kind of knowledge ('ilm) that comes from the "presence of" or "proximity to" God, the Qur'ān offers a parable that helps us better grasp what this knowledge may be. This story finds the Prophet Moses (upon him be peace) and a young servant pursuing a Divine sign, understood in the story to be some kind of elusive fish. As they do so, they run into a most enigmatic person, described simply as "one of Our servants to whom We had given a Mercy from Ourselves and whom We had taught a [special] knowledge from Our own presence." Moses recognizes the profound knowledge in this person and asks him to teach him something of what he knows. What ensues might be described as an initiation into a knowledge that goes deeper than the appearances of things, a knowledge or understanding of a deeper, hidden narrative at work in the superficial story of our experience and perception.

> [Remember] when Moses said to his young servant, "I will not give up until I reach the junction of the two seas or have spent a long time [in pursuit]." But, when the pair reached the junction between the two [seas], they forgot about their great fish, which had taken its way in the sea as though a tunnel. When they had continued on [a while], Moses said to his young servant, "Bring forth our meal, for we have suffered fatigue on account of this journey."
>
> [The servant] said, "Did you see [what happened] when we sought shelter at the rock? I did indeed forget about the great fish. Nothing but Satan caused me to forget to mention it [to you]. It took its course through the sea in an amazing way."
>
> [Moses] said, "That's what we were seeking!" And so they turned back on their tracks, following [the way they had come].

And so they found one of Our servants to whom We had given a Mercy from Ourselves and whom We had taught a [special] knowledge from Our own presence.

Moses said to him: "May I follow you on the condition you teach me something of that which you have been taught by way of true guidance?"

He said, "But surely you will not be able to hold patience with me [if I take you on]. How can you be patient regarding that which is outside of your knowledge [and] experience?"

Moses said: "God willing, you will find me [to be] patient: nor shall I disobey you in any way."

[The Guide] said: "If then you [choose to] follow me, do not ask me about anything until I speak to you about it."

So the two started off [and journeyed] until, as they boarded the boat, [the guide] punched a hole in it. Moses said, "Did you sink it in order to drown those in it? You have done something stupid!"

He said: "Did I not say that you would not be able to remain patient with me?"

Moses said: "Forgive me for forgetting! Do not be excessive in what you demand of me in such difficult circumstances!"

And so the pair set off until they encountered a young man; when they encountered him, [the guide] killed him. [Moses] said, "You have killed an innocent soul without [the death of another] soul [upon him]? You have done something detestable!"

[The guide] replied, "Did I not tell you that you would be unable to hold patience with me?"

[Moses] said, "If I question you about anything after [this], then do not take me as your companion! For you will have won a [solid] excuse from me."

And so the two proceeded . . . when they came to the people of a village, they asked for food, but they [i.e., the inhabitants] refused to treat them [properly] as guests. So the pair found there a wall that was on the point of collapsing. [The guide] then raised it up straight. [Moses] said: "If you had wished, surely you could have taken some payment for [doing] that!"

[The guide] then said, "This is the moment of parting between me and you: [But first] I shall reveal to you the true interpretation (*al-ta'wīl*) of that concerning which you were unable to hold patience.

"As for the boat, it belonged to poor men who worked on the sea. I wanted to make it defective [because] there was behind them a king who was seizing all boats by force.

"As for the young man, his parents were believers, and we dreaded that he would overburden them by oppression [and cruelty] and ingratitude. So we desired that their Lord would give them in exchange one better in purity and closer [to them] in sympathy.

"As for the wall, it belonged to two orphaned youths in the city; [buried] beneath it was a treasure that belonged to them: their father had been a righteous man, and so your Lord wished that the two

[boys], [when] they came of age, find it and excavate their treasure as a mercy from your Lord.

"Thus, I did not do [any of this] of my own [accord]. That, then, is the true interpretation (*al-ta'wīl*) of that concerning which you were unable to hold patience." (Surah of the Cave / *al-Kahf* 18:65–82)

One of the lessons learned here is that there is always more involved in human affairs than meets the eye, and only God understands the full picture. Conventional knowledge or wisdom fails when it tries to judge events and situations by its own standards, and patience (*al-ṣabr*), which in Arabic involves a sense of self-restraint, becomes an essential virtue for transcending the limitations of human knowing and for opening up a space in which Divine knowledge can be imparted. This patience must be accompanied by a disposition of humility, more specifically an epistemological humility, which is understood here and in other passages to be an essential characteristic of the wise person. Indeed, if we read this story in the spirit of *sūra(t) Luqmān* (31), Wisdom here is manifest in the twin virtues of patience and humility.

So, in the parable, Moses—the great prophet who spoke with God directly, who stood against Pharaoh, led the Israelites out of Egypt, and brought forth the Torah—assumes the position of a humble disciple when providence brings him into contact with a person of greater knowledge. True knowledge, then, makes the practical virtues its prerequisites; humility, self-restraint, and patience, along with moral rectitude and the other qualities of the virtuous believer, lead to gnosis. And, even when—like Moses—the virtuous believer fails in those virtues, a flashing of gnosis may be still given, and this gives rise to wisdom.

So we see the interdependence of Truth and Wisdom, of coming to know and being wise. Within the human heart, wisdom seems to include the transformation of one's intellectual and attitudinal disposition after having witnessed Truth, just as we are left to assume that Moses' disposition was radically transformed after this encounter. In other words, embodied, living wisdom comes as a result of witnessing, and this "witnessing" often comes through a personally destabilizing, noetic experience. This destabilization of worldview (and the wisdom that comes after) may be one of the secret reasons why getting to know people of other faiths and ethnicities is, as we will see, nothing less than a Divine imperative clearly voiced in the Qur'ān.

WHY SHARE WISDOM?

Why should Muslims seek to "share" or seek wisdom with and from people of other faiths? What are some of the obstacles to sharing? What are the benefits?

In the Qur'ānic accounts of Luqmān and Moses, we see the importance of both teaching and receiving wisdom. The experience of Truth makes teaching and modeling wisdom imperative, and the call to epistemological humility in the face of the grandeur of Truth makes being humble, patient, and open to instruction equally imperative. The fact that Muslims believe that both Wisdom and Truth have been given to them — through the dispensation of the Qur'ān and the recording of the Prophet Muhammad's words and deeds — does not exempt them from being humble and open to instruction any more than being a prophet exempted Moses from being humble and open to instruction. All Muslims are called to seek Truth, which is a quality of God and thus ever beyond one's current grasp, no matter how brilliant. All Muslims are called to be seekers of Wisdom, which is similarly a quality of God Most High and is thus infinitely within and beyond our reach.

Building upon this interdependence of Truth and Wisdom, the keys to the esoteric, Divine knowledge are said to be found in the identification and deciphering of God's signs (*āyāt*), which are everywhere: in the natural world, in history and the events of our times, in ourselves, and in the sacred texts revealed to humankind throughout history. The Islamic concept of scripture, then, is expansive and all-encompassing, and so the door is left wide open for Muslims to seek God's signs everywhere, even within religious texts and traditions that are foreign to us.

In *sūra(t) āl-'Imrān* / the family of 'Imrān (3), we read:

> Say: "We believe in God, and in what has been revealed to us and what has been revealed to Abraham, and Ishmael, and Isaac, and Jacob, and the Tribes, and in that which was bestowed upon Moses, and Jesus, and the Prophets from their Lord. We make no distinction between anyone among them, and to [God] we surrender." (3:84)

Far from claiming exclusive access to Divine Truth and Wisdom, the Qur'ān celebrates the fact that God, in His mercy benevolence for humankind, has broadcast the message all over the world from the time of Adam on. Indeed, the Qur'ān goes so far as to say that every nation has been sent a messenger.[26] And no message is believed to be complete or exhaustive, for all revelations emanate from a "protected tablet" or "mother book" that resides with God.[27] Even as it proclaims the universal reach of the message in various languages and forms, the Qur'ān also bemoans the fact that humans have repeatedly ignored, resisted, and opposed the teachings of God's messengers; even within the ranks of the believers, it warns that many have turned around and "sold" the priceless signs of God for a miserable gain in the world. For our discussion, the positive side of this oft-repeated Qur'ānic/Biblical story is that God's Truth and Wisdom are believed to be present within the extant remains of the innumerable prophetic dispensations, both oral and written, that have touched every part of the globe.

The most familiar and recurring examples of these authentic teachings can be found in Qur'ānic references to the Torah and the Gospels. For example, in *sūra(t) āl 'imrān* / the family of 'Imrān (3), the Qur'ān says of Jesus:

> And [God] will teach him the Book and the Wisdom and the Law ("al-taurāh" or Torah) and [make him] a messenger to the Children of Israel. (3:48–49)

Also, in *sūra(t) al-mā'idah* / the table (5), the Qur'ān says,

> It was We who revealed the Torah; therein is guidance and light, and by it the Prophets, who surrendered [to God], and the Rabbis made judgments for the Jews . . .
> And in their footsteps We sent Jesus the son of Mary, confirming the Law (Torah) that came before him, and We gave him the Gospel, in which [is] guidance and light and confirmation of the Torah before it, a guidance and an admonition to those who are conscious of God. (5:46)

We find many passages attributing "guidance" and "light" and "wisdom" to the Gospels and the Torah. While a long-standing discussion continues among Muslim scholars over which portions of the existing Torah and Gospels are authentic and which portions show signs of alteration or tampering (*tahrīf*), there can be no overturning the Qur'ānic insistence that these books contain a guidance and a light that endure, and, by extension, so do all of the existing teachings left from God's prophets, who are believed to have been dispersed among the various nations and throughout unnumbered historical periods. The core of what they left behind, according to the Qur'ān, is a belief in God and the last day and a call to upright living, and those who hold fast to the essentials of their message are included among the blessed, the saved:

> Whosoever surrenders himself to God and is [also] a doer of good, he has his reward with his Lord. [On such people] no fear overshadows them, nor do they come to grief. (2:112)

To boil it down to a simple question we pose: can truth and wisdom be sought in other religious texts, traditions, and cultures? The simple Qur'ānic answer seems to be clear.

In this spirit, then, we can note many Muslim intellectuals and wisdom-seekers throughout the centuries, scholars and seekers who made the study of other religions and cultures the defining work of their lives. One of most celebrated of these was the twelfth-century theologian, historian of religious ideas, independent thinker, and theosopher, Muhammad Al-Shahrastānī (Tāj al-Dīn Abū'l-Fath Muhammad ibn 'Abd al-Karīm al-Shahrastānī, d. AH 548 or 1153 CE), who wrote a massive book on the different religious communities and sects known in his day, including all the various intellectual and doctrinal divisions within Islam up to his time. Known in English as *The Book of Religious and Philosophical Sects*,[28] this fascinating text marks an attempt to document and describe, without any detectable bias, condescension, or disrespect of any kind, the religious diversity of humankind. Written many centuries before the rise of Religious Studies as an academic field in the West, his work may just be the very first attempt to undertake the scientific study of religion. More, his work marks a genuine desire to study and learn from religious experiences and histories that were outside of his experience.

In the quest of pursuing God's signs, it can be argued that we too should seek truth and wisdom anywhere and everywhere, including in the perplexing mystery of our religious and ethnic diversity. In *sūra(t) al-mā'idah*, a chapter that stresses the presence of Guidance and Light within the scriptures of the Torah and the Gospel traditions, the Qur'ān states quite clearly that religious diversity and constructive, mutual striving are part of the Divine plan. In *āyah* 48, following a description of how the Qur'ān confirms the scriptures that came before, we read,

> For each [community] have We made a Law (*shar'*) and a Way (*minhāj*); if God had so willed, He could have made you a single community (*ummah*), but [He did not] in order that He might test you in what He has given you. Therefore, race with one another [to do] good works. To God is the return of all of you, and He will make known to you [the truth] of those matters in which you differ.

In this day, dogged as it is with the darknesses of ignorance, prejudice, ethnic cleansing, genocide, terror, and other forms of needless violence and injustice, there can be no doubt that coming to know one another in order to promote healthy coexistence and constructive collaboration for good causes can certainly be counted among the good works intended here, for they are powerful antidotes to the chronic cancers of tumult and oppression in human affairs. More, the Qur'ān seems to allow for some sense of team spirit and competition in the "race" to do good works, an allowance that seems to speak to an important aspect of our human nature.

If further proof or justification is needed to make a case for a hidden Divine purpose in learning about one another and sharing wisdom across traditions, we need only look again to the Qur'ān, this time to *sūra(t) al-hujurāt* / the chambers (49):

> O people! Surely We have created you male and female and have made you [various] nations and tribes in order that you might come to know one another. Indeed, in God's view, the most honorable of you is the most pious. Verily God is Knowing, Expertly Acquainted [with all you do].

From a Qur'ānic perspective, then, both coming to know one another and mutually striving to do good works are clearly part of God's master plan for humanity. The task of getting to know one another comes very close to our contemporary understanding of intercultural and interfaith dialogue, and so—as a Muslim and life-long student of the Islamic tradition—I see dialogue as nothing less than a religious duty, which deepens and enhances my personal piety rather than polluting or diluting it. Racing to perform good works, particularly within a context of being tested with what God has given us, seems to be a broader, more general command that almost certainly encompasses the mutual sharing of the bounties God has bestowed upon us.

Quite apart from God's "sharing" His Wisdom and other Divine qualities with us, this inter-religious or inter-ummah sharing implies a sense of equality, a sense that that each community has been given something of value to share. If done correctly, this should engender a spirit of mutual appreciation whereby by we can marvel at the various treasures of insight and wisdom bestowed upon the individual communities, even as we gain valuable insights into what we share in common.

EXAMPLES OF SHARING IN ISLAMIC HISTORY

As students of Islamic history, we know that one of the chief geniuses of Islamic Civilization was its willingness to learn from the Christians, Jews, Zoroastrians, and other communities living within the rapidly expanding Islamic empire. First, they had practical things to learn. Of course, the Arabs, coming out of the Arabian peninsula, knew little about running a vast empire, and so they turned to the Persian and Greek bureaucracies of the Sassanian and Byzantine empires to educate them. Along the way, as they learned about numismatics, taxation, irrigation, land management, city planning, and a thousand other things hitherto unknown, they also learned how to engineer expansive, dome-roofed buildings and high towers, the two quintessential elements of the emerging mosque standard, and they became enamored with tile manufacturing and a variety of "new" crafts. They also began collecting and translating the medical, astronomical, mathematical, botanical, philosophical lore of the ancient world, and this "new" knowledge empowered them to develop scientific academies and to advance human knowledge beyond any level humanity had ever seen. All this was because they were willing—no, wanting—to receive knowledge from other civilizations and communities.

The Muslims also realized that their non-Muslim counterparts had more profound kinds of knowledge to offer them. Even within the sensitive field of religious knowledge, we find a willingness to receive and learn from the Christians and the Jews. Indeed, an entire branch of Qur'ānic exegesis (*tafsīr*) literature—called the *Isrā'īliyāt*—emerged from such conversations. More, finding themselves surrounded by learned Jews and Christians who had been actively engaged in theological disputation for centuries helped the Muslims develop their own theology (*kalām*), by which they were able to answer theological questions and counter theological attacks. This, of course, helped the Muslims develop the classical creeds and the disciplines of Islamic jurisprudence that have steered the course of Islamic theology and law ever since.

In short, the Muslims historically found themselves immeasurably enriched by the knowledge, experience, and wisdom of other communities and traditions, and the greatness of the civilization they built very much stood upon the shoulders of that sharing. In a way, then, we can see the Muslims actively manifesting the Qur'ānic command to come to know the "other" and to "compete" in the pious race to do good works. Theologically, there is no reason why the same cannot occur and be the norm today.

In this spirit, it is important to acknowledge that the profound richness of this sharing cannot be reduced to domes or minarets or specific scientific insights or theological methods of inquiry, concrete contributions that stand as byproducts rather than ends of coming to know one another. Indeed, the sharing encouraged in the Qur'an and fleshed out in Islamic history is something far richer, for it implies living in relationship with one another, a relationship of regular interaction, collaboration, mutual assistance, and even healthy-minded competition.

OBSTACLES TO INTER-UMMAH SHARING TODAY

Al-Shahrastānī's work was appreciated in his time and has been held in esteem ever since as one of the great achievements of classical Islamic Civilization. Many Muslims today, however, question the need to seek anything—especially Divine Wisdom and Truth—outside the Qur'ān and the other authoritative foundations of the Islamic faith. This somewhat xenophobic attitude, which includes a tangible fear of cultural pollution by "foreign" or non-Islamic elements, has been unwittingly fueled by centuries of western economic, political, and cultural domination. Powerfully championed in the much-quoted works of Sayyid Qutb and others within the self-identified "Salafi" renewal tradition, this religio-political orientation has tremendous appeal in many parts of the traditionally Muslim world, where the West, with its inescapable modernizing and globalizing influences, not to mention its military presence and influence, is viewed with anger and tremendous suspicion.

From such a vantage point, interfaith dialogue (not to mention sharing wisdom)—often seen wrongly as a scheme devised by western Christians and Jews—is frequently accused of being yet another way in which the dominant Western powers seek to impose their own rules and parameters (here relating to religious discourse) upon Muslims and fit Muslim voices into pre-designed roles, where the script is already more-or-less written and just waiting for an "authentic" voice to read it aloud. In this brief chapter, we cannot avoid acknowledging the mistrust many Muslims feel for interfaith dialogue efforts and the post-colonial political, military, social, and psychological factors that continue to enflame this mistrust. These are real and formidable factors that must be examined as we work out a respectful and mutually sensitive way to share with one another as equal partners in the race to do good works.

While overcoming these obstacles may require the work of many generations on all sides, we must do our part to get the process moving forward. The Qur'anic imperative makes this clear, and the deteriorating condition of the planet and the growing hostility between nations make the theological challenge all the more crucial at this moment.

HOW DO WE SHARE?

Again, the close identification of Wisdom with God prevents us from speaking too casually about Wisdom as a commodity or a "something" that can be shared or imparted by one person upon another. The story of Moses and the spirit-guide, however, indicates to us that it is possible for a teacher to help open another's mind or heart to wisdom, and this process seems to include breaking a person out of his or her "normal" way of seeing the world. In the case of Moses, who was repeatedly confronted with situations that could not be grasped with conventional thinking, he was left, perhaps, with the new knowledge that nothing is as it seems, that life cannot be judged at face-value, that there is a deeper meaning or purpose to everything, and that wisdom involves beholding life with a pondering mind and an unwaveringly patient disposition. One will notice that his teacher did not tell him all this in explicit terms; rather, he opened a way for this kind of reflection.

Outside of the teacher-student paradigm, which usually takes place within a single tradition or sub-tradition, is there any sense in which Wisdom can be said to be shared across traditions? Given all that we have said up to this point, the assertion that God's creatures can "share" wisdom with one another may be viewed with suspicion of anthropocentric hubris if taken literally. The more Qur'ānic formulation might be that Wisdom can be mutually sought, pondered, and cherished by the believers of all faith traditions, granted that they come together in all sincerity and with a unifying intention to seek with open minds and hearts. In my reading of the Qur'ānic texts, this seems to be what our Creator intended for us to do in the first place.

ACTIVE SHARING

What does it mean for Muslims to share the wisdom they believe has been given to them? Why share?

Since its inception in the seventh century of the Common Era (CE), Islam has been an evangelical movement that actively sought to "call the world to God" and to "that which gives life." This has often been equated, rightly or wrongly, to converting others to its simple and somewhat uncompromising monotheistic worldview. As it did so, it afforded a place of protection to the religious communities and traditions it recognized as its authentic forbears. Although it began as a small, unpopular, extremely disadvantaged movement within a dominant culture of polytheism and relative lawlessness within the Arabian Peninsula, the movement rapidly grew powerful under the Prophet's leadership and went on to establish an impressive and vast empire soon after his death. Thus, one of the ways in which Muslims have actively shared and still share today is through the teaching of their faith to others and through the promotion of a general culture that champions the sanctification of the public sphere in addition to the theatres of our individual hearts and personal lives. This sanctification manifests itself, in part, through a Divinely-inspired legal tradition that seeks to protect religious minorities and provide for the disadvantaged as it sets an overarching moral and ethical standard for the marketplace and larger society.

This active sharing came easily and naturally when the Muslim empires were politically, economically, technologically, culturally, and militarily supreme, for the beauty of their cities, the civility of their societies, and the erudition of their academies proclaimed their wisdom to the wider world in very compelling ways. Indeed, during the "golden" centuries of Islamic Civilization, the Muslims were so confident and secure that they were able to share and collaborate with all kinds of cultures and religious groups.

The situation today, however, is dramatically different, and Muslims are being forced to rethink their traditional modes of sharing. How can we share wisdom when we are politically, economically, militarily, and culturally compromised? How can we share wisdom when we are despised in the popular media in so many countries, especially in the west? Apart from converting everyone, what do we have to offer the wider world? Are there ways Muslims can share their wisdom humbly, as global partners with peoples of other faiths, or can such sharing only occur when Islam is recognized as the unrivalled superior in every sense? Are there ways in which Muslims can actively enrich others with traditional Islamic wisdom without seeking to convert them or at least win them over to a more balanced and appreciative understanding of Islam and Muslims?

RECEIVING WISDOM

Of course, this process need not be understood as a homogenizing experience, where our uniqueness is compromised or threatened in any way. There will always be particular perceptions of Wisdom that do not—and cannot—transcend the boundaries of our faith traditions. This is certainly true for Muslims, who see the Qur'ān as abrogating all earlier sacred texts, no matter how esteemed and luminous and salvifically valid, and understand the Prophet Muhammad to be the final messenger sent to humankind before the end of the world as we know it and the advent of Judgment Day. These beliefs are both unique and essential to the religion of Islam and so cannot be "shared" beyond an informational level. Other religious traditions likewise have their own examples of "unshareable" wisdoms, and we have to be comfortable with this. We should think, then, about the wisdoms we can share more fully. What can Islam bring to such a banquet?

For starters, I think Muslims can bring a reverence and a humility to this discussion, the reverence emanating from the awareness that wisdom truly is of God and from God, that we are seeking to share the gifts bestowed upon us from the Giver of Bounty (*al-Wahhāb*); the humility arises also from our remembrance of Moses and from our explicit awareness that our understanding of these treasures is incomplete and partial at best. These offerings are absolutely authentic to the Islamic tradition and may serve the overall spirit in which we, as peoples of different communities, share.

LOVE AND FORGIVENESS: SHARING WISDOM FROM THE QURAN

As is the case with Wisdom itself, Love and Forgiveness are qualities of God, and so we are forced to wrestle again with transcendence as we attempt to enter into a theoretical and experiential discourse that can serve our situations and our needs. In the brief glimpses of love and forgiveness that we have already explored above, we see that these two Divine qualities are often connected with one another and also with the transformation of the individual (or community) involved. This aspect of transformation is crucial for understanding why the Qur'ānic texts stress forgiveness in human interactions; indeed, the Qur'ān even explains this in the story of Yūsuf (Joseph) and his brothers, as we will see below.

Of the ninety-nine attributes or "beautiful names" of God in the Qur'ān, at least six reflect different aspects of God's forgiveness and mercy, and these also happen to be among the most repeated names of God in the sacred text. It should be no surprise, therefore, that both the Qur'ān and the Prophetic traditions treat forgiveness, forbearance, clemency, mercy, and reconciliation as hallmark characteristics of the true believers.[29] The role models for these virtues are typically the prophets, and so we turn now to their stories in our search for Islamic wisdom concerning forgiveness.

As has been mentioned in some of my earlier writings,[30] one of the most beautiful and moving accounts of forgiveness in the Qur'ān comes from "the most beautiful of stories," the story of Yūsuf (Joseph) and his brothers. Found in the twelfth chapter or *sūrah* of the Qur'an, this is an epic story of innocence betrayed, envy, violence, injustice, long-suffering, patience, and ultimate exaltation in a scene of recognition, repentance, and unexpected forgiveness on both human and Divine levels. Joseph says to his brothers, "Today there is no blame on you. God will forgive [everything] for you. He is the Most Merciful of all those who show mercy."

Inspired by Joseph's clemency and the promise of God's forgiveness, they go back to their father, Jacob, whose sight has been restored by the casting of Joseph's shirt over his face.

> They said, "O our father! Ask [God] to forgive our sins, for verily we were sinners!"
>
> [Jacob] said, "I will seek the forgiveness of my Lord for you, for He is indeed the Oft-Forgiving, the Merciful."
>
> Then when they entered the presence of Joseph, he made a home for his parents with himself and said, "[I bid] you enter Egypt, by God's leave, with safety."
>
> And he raised his parents high on the throne, and they [all] fell down in prostration before him. He said, "O my father! This is the meaning of my vision of old! God has made it true! He was indeed good to me when freed me from prison and brought you [all] here from the desert after Satan had put enmity between me and my brothers. Truly my Lord is Subtle [in unveiling] whatever He wills! Verily He is the Knowing, the Wise." (12:90–100)

The brothers are transformed, as is their situation, and they are now reconciled with their brother. The envy they had once felt and the evil it had once inspired are all placed upon Satan, even they take full responsibility for their crimes. Love and forgiveness triumph, and the story ends with a resounding spirit of gratitude for God's goodness. Everyone is redeemed.

With significant changes of scenery and circumstance, this same dynamic is played out in the life of the Prophet Muhammad. After years of waging a war to wipe out Muhammad and his Companions, along with their monotheistic movement that threatened the pre-Islamic pilgrimage (and all of the commercial success it generated) in Mecca, the people of Mecca were defenseless and at his mercy. Fearing the worst, they entreated him to be merciful after he had asked, "what do you think I shall do to you now?" Then, thinking of Joseph, he is reported to have answered his own question: "Today I shall say to you what Joseph said to his brothers: 'Today there is no blame on you.' Go, you are all free."

This act of mercy and forgiveness inspired the people of Mecca to embrace Islam. The "House of God" (the Ka'ba) was cleared and renewed as a center for Abrahamic, monotheistic devotion. The clemency of God had become palpably manifest in their midst, and the immediate result was the reunification of families and the forward march of an expanded and united Muslim community.

The wisdom that Muslims can and should share regarding forgiveness, then, is simply that, even when grave injustices have been perpetrated and serious injury incurred, forgiveness opens a path toward reconciliation and renewal. This follows the pattern that God has decreed for Godself as well as the pattern modeled in the beautiful stories of Joseph and Muhammad. If we are to listen to the wisdom of the Islamic tradition, from the inter-relation of the Divine attributes to the stories of the prophets, including the life of the Prophet Muhammad, we hear a call to restrain our anger, however justified, to forgive those who have harmed us, and to step forward into a future of new and unforeseen possibility. This is what it must mean to be wise, to live in the transformed state of those who live in witness to Truth.

NOTES

1. Unless otherwise noted, all translations from the Qur'an are the author's own.
2. See, for example, 2:231; 3:48, 81; 4:113; 5:110; 10:1; 19:12; 31:2; 33:34; 36:2; 38:20; 43:4; 62:2.
3. See, for example, 31:2.
4. 3 See 2:30, 35, 255; 16: 77; 18:26; 25:6; 49:18.
5. Al-Ghazālī, *The Ninety-Nine Beautiful Names of God*, trans. with notes by David B. Burrell and Nazih Daher (Islamic texts Society, 1992, 1995), 117.
6. 21:74.
7. 21:12.
8. 2:251; 27:15.
9. 3:48–49.
10. 19:12.
11. 2:269; 29:49; 58:11.
12. See, for example, *sūra(t) al-anbiyā'* / the prophets (21): 24.
13. 2: 269; 3:7.
14. 3:7.
15. Al-Ghazālī, *The Ninety-Nine Beautiful Names of God*, 117.
16. 46:23.
17. 95:4.
18. See, for example, 2:34 and following.
19. See Al-Ghazālī, *The Ninety-Nine Beautiful Names of God*, 30–45.
20. See Al-Ghazālī, *The Ninety-Nine Beautiful Names of God*, 149–56.
21. See William Chittick, trans., *Faith and Practice of Islam: Three Thirteenth Century Sufi Texts* (Albany: State University of New York Press, 1992), 54–56.
22. From the *Ṣaḥīḥ* collection of al-Bukhārī (vol. 8, Book 75). Another tradition, also recorded in al-Bukhārī's catalogue, runs, "God has ninety-nine names, i.e., one hundred minus one; whoever recounts them will enter paradise."
23. See the entirety of *sūrah* 31.
24. 16:77; 49:18; 18:26; 25:6.
25. Exactly what these "names" pertain to remains something of a mystery. In some Islamic texts, they are taken to be the Divine names or attributes, while, in others, they are seen as having to do with the essential natures of everything to be found within

the created realm, of which Adam is seen as the primordial steward or vicegerent (*khalīfa*). See, for example, Ibn al-'Arabī, *The Bezels of Wisdom*, trans. & intro. by R. W. J. (Austin, TX: Paulist Press, 1980), 50–59.

26. 10:47.

27. 13:39; 43:4.

28. William Cureton, ed. (Gorgias Press, 2002). A fully annotated French translation of the book, sponsored by UNESCO and undertaken by Daniel Gimaret, Guy Monnot and Jean Jolivet and can be found under the title, *Shahrastani: Livre des religions et des sects* (Leuven: Peeters, 1986, 1993).

29. See, for example, 42:37; 42:40; 16:126–127; 24:22.

30. See my chapter, "Muslim Leadership: Past, Present, Future" in *The Future of Religious Leadership: World Religions in Conversation*, ed. Alon Goshen-Gottstein (Lanham, MD: Lexington Books, 2016), 73–74.

SIX
A Jewish Perspective

Meir Sendor

WHAT IS WISDOM?

Jewish texts and thinkers, when expressing themselves technically, distinguish between wisdom and revelation and make corresponding distinctions between what is appropriate for sharing between Jews and those outside the Jewish community and what is not. The foundation of Jewish tradition is divine revelation, cognitive content communicated directly from God to human beings. Transmitted prophetically, this content comprises the legal, moral and spiritual substance of Torah and the prophetic tradition, and issuing from God it is inherently true and transcendently wise. Wisdom, by contrast, is regarded as an essentially human activity, the effort to process divine revelation with human experience, to understand the world and human existence, though this effort itself can be divinely inspired.[1]

While this distinction is implicit in certain biblical texts,[2] it begins to come more sharply into relief in rabbinic texts of the Talmudic period, where the further distinction is made between "the wisdom of Israel" and "the wisdom of the nations."[3]

> Behold I have taught you statutes and laws as the Lord my God commanded me, to do accordingly in the midst of the land that you are going to, to inherit. Observe them and do them, for it is your wisdom and understanding in the eyes of the nations, who will hear all these statutes and say: surely a wise and understanding people is this great nation. (Deut. 4:5, 6)

Medieval commentators such as Rashi and R. Avraham Ibn Ezra take this passage broadly: that the wisdom of the statutes and laws of the Torah will be apparent to other nations and admired by them. These verses, taken in their plain sense, indicate an expectation of some communication between Jews and non-Jews on issues of law and religion, and a polemical concern to foster a positive attitude among non-Jews towards Jews and Jewish wisdom[4]. They elaborate on the distinction between "the wisdom of the Torah," the result of interpreting the divine revelation of Torah and correlating it with life experience, and "other wisdoms" which result from the general human effort to understand the world, human existence and the horizons of human consciousness.[5] It is in this category of "other wisdoms," also classified as "external wisdoms," that some traditional Jewish thinkers find common ground and a basis for mutual sharing between Jews and non-Jewish cultures.[6] Torah and "the wisdom of Torah" are regarded as an exclusively Jewish preserve,[7] and whatever limited cross-cultural sharing of this truth and wisdom may occur is strictly one way, from Jews to non-Jews.[8]

Jewish tradition has another way of speaking about wisdom, not as cognitive content, but as an intellectual posture. In the Mishnah tractate Avot 4:1 "Ben Zoma says, 'Who is wise? One who learns from every human being.'" The statement is intentionally ironic. One expects the wise person to be defined as someone in possession of a substantial repertoire of knowledge. Ben Zoma's point is that wisdom is actually an attitude, a broad and self-effacing openness to learning and receiving insight from everyone—not just from Jews or sages, but from "every human being." Rabbenu Jonah Gerondi (1200–1263) develops this theme of wisdom and understanding as an attitude of intellectual humility in his Commentary on Proverbs:

> "Wisdom is before the face of one who understands (Proverbs 17:24)." We have already explained the issue of an understanding person, that he loves to understand words of wisdom and he has the heart to understand them. If one of these factors is missing, he is not called understanding . . . For if there are no people great in wisdom in his locale, he will inquire of every person that which he knows, and learn from every human being. What prompts this in him is his love of wisdom. Therefore he submits himself to learn from every human being, whether great or small, and he accepts the truth from whoever says it.

The point is that the ideal attunement to wisdom is reckoned not just, or even primarily, in terms of knowledge possessed, but in terms of an attitude of receptivity that welcomes and pursues mutual sharing among all seekers of truth.

WHY SHARE WISDOM?

Mutual sharing of wisdom with other cultures is inherently challenging for a tradition based on divine revelation, a body of revelatory life wisdom regarded as complete and perfect. Jewish authorities from the Talmudic period to the present cite biblical verses and rabbinic comments to the effect that the content and methodology of Torah tradition is entirely self-sufficient.[9] Theoretically, whatever sharing of wisdom this position openly acknowledges would be unilateral, in terms of what Judaism can offer the world. For such authorities, even this sharing tends to be limited to just those elements of law and ethics relevant to non-Jewish behavior, or tends to be deferred entirely to the eschatological Messianic Age.

> And it shall come to pass in the last days, that the mountain of the Lord's house shall be established on the tops of the mountains and shall be exalted above the hills, and all nations shall flow to it. And many people shall go and say, Come, and let us go up to the mountain of the Lord, to the house of the God of Jacob, and He will teach us of His ways and we will walk in His paths, for out of Zion shall go forth Torah, and the word of God from Jerusalem. (Isaiah 2:23)

In this prophecy, the eschatological ideal is expressed in terms wisdom and knowledge: the universal desire of all nations to learn from Israel about God and His ways. Maimonides further describes:

> The sages did not long for the days of the Messiah in order to rule over the whole world, nor to subdue the idolators, nor to be exalted by the nations, nor to eat and drink and rejoice, but rather that they should be free to engage in Torah and its wisdom, that there should be no one to oppress or hinder them, in order that they should attain the life of the World to Come, as we have explained in the laws of Repentance.
>
> In that time there will be no famine and no war, no jealousy and no conflict. Good will be bestowed abundantly, and all kinds of delicacies available as dust. The pursuit of the whole world will be nothing other than to know God alone. Therefore Israelites will be great sages, knowing the hidden things and attaining knowledge of their Creator according to human capacity, as it says "The earth shall be full with the knowledge of the Lord as the waters cover the sea (Is. 11:9)."[10]

The ideal way of life of the Messianic era is expressed in terms of the universal sharing of wisdom among all human beings. There is a delicacy and restraint in the way Maimonides describes the position of Torah in this enlightened world culture: Israelites and Torah wisdom will have high standing, but there is no imposition of Torah or Jewish tradition as an exclusive system upon those who are not Jewish.

The view that affirms the Torah's self-sufficiency finds classic Rabbinic articulation in Mishnah Avot 5:22: "Ben Bag Bag says 'turn it over, turn it over, for all is in it; in it you will attain vision; grow old and exhaust yourself in it; from it do not depart, for you have no better value than it.'" The notion is that the Torah contains all wisdom, and that this can be discovered through sustained and diligent investigation and exclusive focus on Torah study as a life-long commitment.[11] This very text, however, raises a methodological question regarding the approach to wisdom. The comprehensive self-sufficiency of Torah is not explicit, it requires turning over, investigation, interpretation. From where does one acquire the skills and sensibilities to ask the penetrating questions of Torah so as to discover in it all wisdom? R. Moses Almosnino (c.1515—c.1580) addresses the repetition "turn it over, turn it over":

> The first refers to engaging in Torah itself, the second, that one should engage, through it, in everything else. That is, when one studies other disciplines, he will relate them to it, so that he will strive to harmonize what he learns with what is written in the Torah . . . For it is impossible that you should say that Torah and other sciences are separate, for everything is in it.[12]

His point is that the process of turning over and interpreting the Torah proceeds together with a wide-ranging engagement with all knowledge.[13] R. Almosnino, of distinguished Sefardic lineage, reflects a line of thought central in medieval Judeo-Spanish and Provençal culture that welcomed a harmonizing synthesis between Jewish and non-Jewish wisdom in philosophy and the sciences.

Some thinkers took the synthesis beyond mere harmonization. For instance, R. Yedaiah Bedersi (1270–1340), writing to support the study of philosophy when it was challenged by other Provencal and Spanish rabbinic leaders during the Maimonidean Controversy of the turn of the fourteenth century, observed:

> In the early generations, the corporeal conception of God spread through virtually the entire Jewish exile . . . However, in all generations there arose Geonim and sages in Spain, Babylonia and the cities of Andalusia, who, because of their expertise in the Arabic language, encountered the great propaedeutic knowledge that comes with smelling the scent of the various forms of wisdom, whether to a greater or lesser degree, which have been translated into that language. Consequently, they began to clarify many opinions in their study of Torah, especially with regard to the unity of God and the rejection of corporeality, with particular use of philosophical proofs taken from the speculative literature.[14]

To understand R. Bedersi, we turn to Maimonides' *Mishne Torah*:

> It is well known and clear that the love of the Holy One, blessed be He, is not bound in a person's heart until he meditates on it constantly as is appropriate and abandons everything in the world except for this, as it says "[You shall love the Lord your God] with all you heart and all your soul (Deut 6:5)." A person cannot love God except according to

the knowledge by which he knows Him. According to the knowledge will be the love: if a little, then a little; if a lot, then a lot. Therefore a person must dedicate himself to understand and gain insight concerning those wisdoms and understandings which inform him of his Creator, according to a person's capacity to understand and to grasp, as we have explained in the laws of the Foundations of the Torah.[15]

Returning to R. Yedaiah Bedersi, he goes so far as to say that not only is there precedent in Jewish tradition for openness to wisdom from other cultures, but that Hellenistic philosophic and scientific wisdom translated into Arabic had helped Jews of the tenth to twelfth centuries to clarify their own core religious principles. Sharing wisdom with other cultures may stimulate us to ask penetrating questions of our own tradition, to help us come to a deeper understanding of elements, even central elements, we may have previously overlooked or taken for granted. The challenge of wisdom from other religious cultures may rouse a religious community from intellectual stagnation, self-delusion and decline.

This methodological approach was formulated more explicitly and normatively by R. Elijah b. Solomon, the Gaon of Vilna (1720–1797), one of the most accomplished and revered Torah scholars of the early modern period. He is quoted by R. Barukh Schick of Shklov (d. 1808) in the latter's introduction to his book on geometry: "When I visited Vilna in Tevet 5538 (1778) . . . I heard from the holy lips of the Gaon of Vilna that to the extent one is deficient in other wisdoms he will be deficient a hundredfold in Torah study, for Torah and wisdom are bound up together."[16] The Vilna Gaon emphasized that, in order to appreciate the wisdom of Torah, a broad and deep study of other wisdoms is necessary: other wisdoms contribute to developing a proper knowledge base for Torah study itself.

A relatively recent approach to a theory of global wisdom that would account for how a tradition based on divine revelation would be open to, or even require, a mutual sharing of wisdom with other cultures, was articulated by R. Abraham Isaac Kook (1865–1935), first Ashkenazi Chief Rabbi of Israel during the Mandate period. According to R. Kook:

> God has been charitable with His world by not placing all aptitudes in one place, not in one person and not in one nation, not in one land, not in one generation nor in one world. Rather, aptitudes are scattered, and the need for wholeness, which is the most idealistic attracting power, motivates the pursuit of the most exalted unity, which must necessarily come to the world, "and in that day the Lord will be one and His Name one." (Zech 14:9)
>
> The eternal treasury of the virtue of Israel is hidden. But to unite the world with them in a general sense it is necessary that certain aspects of certain aptitudes be lacking in Israel, such that they be made whole by the world and all the noble ones of the nations. In this way there is a place for a receptivity in Israel to receive from the world. As a conse-

> quence the way is open for influence, though receptivity is external and influence is internal. This is to say that the innerness of life is whole in Israel, without need for assistance from any alien power in the world, and all power of dominion in Israel flows from the innerness of life, "from the midst of your brethren—from the most distinguished of your brethren" (Baba Kama 88a on Deut. 17:15). It is regarding the externality of life that it occurs that fulfillment is necessary specifically from the outside, "the beauty of Yafet in the tents of Shem (Megillah 9b on Gen. 9:27)," "the valor of the nations you shall consume, and by their glory you shall be exalted" (Is. 61:6). From the flow of the innerness of life the Congregation of Israel only influences, never receives, "the Lord set him apart, and with him is no strange deity." (Deut. 32:12)[17]

R. Kook lays out a theory and theology of the sharing of wisdom: that by divine plan each nation is granted certain aptitudes and certain deficiencies, so that by necessity nations must interrelate to develop a collective wholeness and unity. Through this concept of divinely ordained deficiency, R. Kook addresses the inclination of nations and their associated religious systems, especially those founded on revelation, to regard themselves as perfect and self-sufficient. This necessary interdependence also applies to Israel and its place among the nations. R. Kook distinguishes, however, between receptivity and influence. The point is that at its core, in its ownmost essence, Israel is self-sufficient as a nation; it can be receptive, but not subject to abject influence. Rabbi Kook roots his discussion in a verse that has a history of rabbinic interpretation condoning cooperative sharing of wisdom between "the tents of Shem," progenitor of the Semites and of Israel, and "the beauty of Yafet," progenitor of Greece and Hellenism.

R. Kook acknowledges that sharing of information between cultures is necessary, and the danger of destabilizing influence is therefore always possible. When sharing is responsible, however, receptivity is limited to peripheral matters, while the core of Israel's culture and religion remains intact and impervious to abject influence.

R. Kook gives a further rationale for the mutual sharing of wisdom between Israel and the nations: not just as filling a deficit, but for the sake of cultivating a peaceful, loving symbiotic relationship among all nations that issues in a higher synergy:

> Concerning the other religions I will state to your honor my opinion, that it is not the aim of the enlightenment that emanates from Israel to absorb or destroy them, just as it is not our aim to destroy the world's different nationalities. Our aim is rather to perfect them and to elevate them, to purge them of their dross. Then they will automatically be joined to the root of Israel, which will exert on them an enlightening influence.[18]

R. Kook envisions the role of Israel among the nations as affirming the best of each nation's unique genius, helping to perfect, elevate and sanctify it according to the principles of Jewish ethics and spirituality. He goes on to explain that this engagement with the wisdom of other nations is ultimately for the sake of promoting love and understanding among all nations.

HOW IS WISDOM SHARED?

The experience of the Jewish people with other world religious communities has been conditioned externally by a complex set of socio-political and cultural pressures, and internally by a principled resistance to overt syncretism. Our tumultuous history includes the struggle to survive in the ever-volatile Derekh ha-Yam, or Via Maris region of the Middle East, crossroads between the powerful civilizations of Egypt and Mesopotamia; the struggle to maintain identity and integrity through exile, diaspora and persecution among often hostile host cultures; and the challenges that the more open societies of the contemporary West pose to a minority culture. Through all this, the Jewish approach to other cultures has never had the luxury of merely indulging benign curiosity or offering the confident, generous welcome of a settled and secure nation-state. Rather, the Jewish relation to other cultures and their religious ideologies has often been urgent, imposed, inescapable and dangerous, and this historical experience of vulnerability has impacted Jewish attitudes and approaches to the sharing of wisdom with other religious communities.

In certain historical circumstances and communities, the prevailing Jewish attitude to other religions and cultures is defensive: an attempt to define one's own character over against other, often dominant, religious cultures perceived as spiritually pernicious and morally corrupt. In other circumstances and communities, Jews express a positive attitude or even drive to understand other religions and their insights, and work to integrate what they learn within the authentic framework of Jewish tradition. Even in periods of general defensiveness, however, there is often a significant degree of receptivity, all the more probative of cultural pressure because it may be subliminal and unacknowledged. Conversely, in periods of general openness, there are instinctively wary counter-attitudes that work to maintain boundaries and preserve authenticity. The attitude to other religious cultures and wisdoms is one of the pivotal distinctions between contemporary Jewish Orthodoxy, which tends to be cautious and protective, and the more liberal Reform and Conservative movements.

Generally speaking, Jewish communities, imbedded in other cultures through most of their history, have always been sharing information with their non-Jewish neighbors, even when relations were chilly or hostile. In the Talmud there is abundant evidence that rabbinic thinkers were fully aware of the non-Jewish societies among whom they lived, and commented, approvingly or disapprovingly, on their moral and intellectual qualities.[19] There is further evidence of Jewish engagement in scientific discussions showing an awareness of non-Jewish positions on the issues. In certain cases, the rabbinic authorities demonstrate their intellectual honesty, deciding that the non-Jewish positions are more cogent than their own.[20] We also have evidence of actual discussions and mutual sharing between Jewish and non-Jewish leaders on subjects dealing with scientific and even spiritual wisdom.[21]

More integral examples of receptivity in sharing wisdom can be found in authoritative medieval Jewish thinkers who systematically incorporated non-Jewish ideas into their works, not just on matters of natural science peripheral to Jewish religion and wisdom, but in the very heart of Jewish theology. Maimonides (1135–1204), for instance, in the Mishneh Torah, his monumental legal code, discusses divine knowledge and unity using the following formulation:

> The Holy One, Blessed be He, recognizes His truth and knows it as it is. He does not know by a knowledge that is external to Him, the way we know. For we and our knowledge are not one. But for the Creator, blessed be He, He and his knowledge and His life are one, from every side and every angle and in every manner of oneness. . . . It turns out that one can say that He is the Knower, He is the Known and He is the Knowing, all one. This thing the mouth has not the power to express, nor the ear to hear, nor the heart of a person to recognize it clearly. . . . Therefore, since He knows Himself He knows all, for all is dependent on Him in His existence.[22]

Maimonides' discussion of divine knowledge and unity employs contemporary Aristotelian and Muslim attribute theory conflated with the rigorous demands of Jewish philosophical monotheism. His description of the nature of divine knowledge, that God is the Knower, the Known and the Knowing, paraphrases Aristotle's speculation on the nature of divine activity in Metaphysics, 12:9, that God is the thinker, the object of thought and the act of thinking. That Maimonides includes this philosophically sophisticated discussion in his Jewish legal code, a text intended for every Jew, demonstrates his complete internalization of the cross-cultural philosophic wisdom of his time, and his confidence that this synthesis should be normative for the Jewish community. That Maimonides uses an Aristotelian formula to express the very heart of his most sublime understanding of God as One is eloquent testimony to his vision of the cross-cultural commonality of wisdom at the very highest levels. Once Maimonides and other authoritative thinkers render such philosophical ideas and terminology mainstream, one finds them appearing in the works of later thinkers, ironically even among those who take essentially rejectionist stands against sharing wisdom.[23]

RESPONSIBLE SHARING OF WISDOM

The Jewish scholarly tradition is acutely sensitive to cultivating the proper conditions for sharing wisdom, inside and outside the Jewish community. Wisdom is not a commodity to be poured from one container to another. It is a shaping of mind, and its sharing involves an intimate, mutual interpenetration of consciousness, calling for great delicacy and mutual respect. The teacher-student relationship is the heart of Jewish life, and careful attention is given to the level of preparation necessary for the student to receive and the level of mastery required for the teacher to teach.[24] These demands within the Jewish community also condition Jewish approaches to respectful sharing with those outside the Tradition.

The sharing of wisdom between cultures risks certain dangers. A premature, uninformed and uncritical sense of commonality can lead to an inauthentic syncretism and generalization, to false assumptions of sameness, obscuring important distinctions between faiths. For example, the notion of a common Judeo-Christian tradition often overlooks the distinctive and decisive influence of Roman religion on early Christianity, which conditions its theology and leads to theological and ethical principles that differ significantly and essentially from Judaism. Similarly, a lack of discernment regarding the subtleties of the Jewish understanding of one God can lead to an uncritical assumption that monotheism is understood identically across Judaism, Christianity, Islam and some forms of Hinduism. In the same vein, the Jewish understanding of the hiddenness of God and the insistence on non-representational theology is not merely an anti-aesthetic, and not even just an epistemological principle, but also stands as a fundamental ethical guarantee of the personal reality of God as transcendent, infinite Other. Reaching for relationship with God's Otherness, hidden and therefore irreducible, incomparable and real, sensitizes us to the mystery of relationship with all others, also irreducible and real in their own ways. Missing this point has led to misguided attempts to see certain commonalities between theistic Judaism and non-theistic, non-personal Buddhist thought. Such examples of syncretism distort our sense of the other and of ourselves.

Sharing wisdom is also an exercise in translation, and much can be lost in the process. Wisdom does not merely reside in the words used to express it. When conveyed without context and full cultural deconstruction, the results can be misleading and misunderstood.

There is also the possibility of a lack of parity in sharing between a dominant host culture and a subordinate guest culture. A dominant culture can even, over time, divert a subordinate culture from its ownmost course in subtle and surreptitious, as well as overt and intentional ways. For instance, the demand of logical consistency and the approach to ontology as a search for commonality, both fundamental attitudes of Hellenism,[25] have influenced medieval and modern Jewish thinkers to limit the sense of God to abstract and psychological terms, losing touch with the vital sense of God conveyed by the Torah, Prophets and Wisdom literature of the Bible. According to Polysystem theory, however, even when there is a power imbalance between cultures, the subordinate culture tends to absorb only those aspects of the host culture that resonate with its own core meaning structure.[26]

The question of responsible sharing between Jewish and non-Jewish faith communities was addressed by R. Joseph B. Soloveitchik (1903–1993), leading Talmudist and philosopher of Modern Orthodox Jewry, and my revered teacher. Responding in 1964 to increased interfaith contacts between Jews and Catholics during the years of the Second Vatican Council, R. Soloveitchik set guidelines and limits on inter-religious discussion and activity. He insisted on two points: that Judaism be valued on its own terms, not as a precursor superseded by other faiths; and that sharing of wisdom be limited:

> The discussion should concern itself not with theological but with secular matters of mutual concern. In the private religious realm, each faith has its own "words" and forms which are uniquely intimate, reflecting its philosophical character, and are totally incomprehensible to people of other faiths. The claims of supernatural experiences on the part of each group differ, and an attempt to achieve dialogue on this level can cause more friction than amity, more confusion than clarity, and thereby prove harmful to the interrelationship. The areas of joint concern should be outer-oriented, to combat the secularism, materialism and atheistic negation of religion and religious values which threaten the moral underpinnings of our society. As far as religion is concerned, we should be guided by the words of Micah (4:5): "Let all people walk, each one in the name of its god, and we shall walk in the name of the Lord, our God, for ever and ever."
>
> Our approach to the outside world has always been of an ambivalent character. We cooperate with members of other faiths in all fields of human endeavor, but, simultaneously, we seek to preserve our distinct integrity which inevitably involves aspects of separateness. This is a paradoxical situation. Yet, paraphrasing the words of our first ancestor, Abraham, we are very much residents in general human society, while, at the same time, strangers and outsiders in our persistent endeavor to preserve our historic religious identity.[27]

Rav Soloveitchik is concerned to counter certain attitudes he detects among some Jewish and Catholic participants. To maintain the religious integrity of all parties in interfaith contacts, R. Soloveitchik suggests that the participants avoid discussions of theology and spiritual experience, which cannot be authentically translated from one religious community to another, and instead focus on moral, social and political areas of common cause among all religions, including combating secularism and materialism and their consequent immorality. He argues that the goal of interfaith relations should be to maintain the fruitful multiplicity and distinctiveness of all religions, rather than an attempt to enforce a unity that does violence to the integrity of each faith.

Reflecting on Rav Soloveitchik's position, one wonders: Does all spiritual experience occur within an immediate or already-present interpretive context that is particular to a specific religious community and inaccessible to others? Or do the core experiences around which a religion coalesces, experiences approaching the horizons of shared human consciousness, have a raw, pre-interpretive dimension offering the possibility of some common ground for some degree of careful and delicate sharing and critical, fully-deconstructed comparison?[28] While the "words," "forms," and "claims" of a religion, its interpretive tradition, are difficult to communicate, or even "incomprehensible" outside the tradition, one might yet pose a phenomenological question regarding spiritual experience itself. Can there be value in sharing wisdom at this level, not only for promoting social and political harmony, worthy goals in themselves, but even for meaningful, cooperative human spiritual exploration?

Examples of Jewish Reception of Wisdom

Western philosophy and science have had a profound impact on Jewish thought from the Hellenistic period to the present. Despite efforts to resist, the content and method of the Hellenistic approach to reality has been appropriated by many Jewish thinkers as a means of articulating the Jewish world view, while they have attempted, at the same time, to preserve a distinctive Jewish spirit. The Hellenistic standard of logical consistency and a mind-body dualism that favors mind over body have influenced Jewish thought and attitudes, even though they are alien to the more non-systematic and holistic spirit of biblical Judaism. This has influenced Jewish piety from the Talmudic period to the present and has even affected the way in which Jews have come to envision God, as more closely associated with the realm of abstract intellect, as opposed to the unlimited, vital and spontaneous sense of the reality of God conveyed by the Bible.

Examples of Jewish Wisdom Given

Despite its embattled position through most of its history of exile and diaspora, and perhaps because of it, the Jewish People has had considerable impact on other world religions and cultures. The most significant gift of the Jewish people to the world is the Bible itself, the most widely read, published and translated book on the planet, a work that has had profound influence on all Western religions, whose narratives and historical vision and whose legal, ethical and spiritual principles, are woven deeply into Western consciousness.

The principle of the oneness of God has been echoed in Christianity, Islam and the Sikh tradition, each in their own ways. In Judaism, this is not just a theological idea, it is also an ethical principle: the transcendent, absolute unity of God, as understood in Judaism, subtends all reality, and transcendently embraces all beings.[29] This is the basis for the responsibility of all human beings for each other, for all creatures and for the world as a whole, and it is the ground for the possibility of love and forgiveness and the overcoming of animosities between individuals and cultures.

LOVE AND FORGIVENESS, SPECIAL EXAMPLES OF JEWISH WISDOM GIVEN

A major gift of Jewish tradition to world religion and civilization is the conviction of the integral relation of law and ethics, that the inner spirit of the law is the ethical ideal. This finds its most succinct expression a rabbinic discussion in the Jerusalem Talmud tractate Nedarim 9:4: "It is taught: Rabbi Akiva says 'You shall love your neighbor as yourself (Lev. 19:18),' is the great principle of the Torah. Ben Azzai says: 'This is book of the generations of man [in the day God created man, in the likeness of God He created him (Gen. 5:1)]' is a greater principle than that." According to Rabbi Akiva, the entire legal structure of the Torah, justice with compassion, is based upon the principle of mutual love and constitutes a call to recognize that love and realize it. According to Ben Azzai, even that principle of ethical relationship is too limited: in the verse cited, love of the other is limited to relative parity with love of self, and love of the other is limited to your neighbor. Ben Azzai cites another verse as expressing an even more fundamental principle: that all humanity is created in the image of the divine. As such, the love and respect and responsibility due to every other human being are not relative to oneself but absolute, and this is the inner principle of all Torah law.[30]

The possibility of mutual love among all human beings, and the demand to realize this ideal, finds concrete expression in the Jewish conception of forgiveness. The ground for the possibility of forgiveness is the generosity of God expressed through the world He creates and guides: that there is a resilience to life, and healing is possible. While the Jewish conception of forgiveness has had resonance in Christianity, the Jewish approach to forgiveness remains different from the Christian approach in theory and in practice. For Jews, forgiveness is not granted a priori, it must be earned by the hard work of apology, compensatory justice and reconciliation.

The Jewish approach to forgiveness requires that responsibility be taken for injury. This is different, for instance, from contemporary "truth and reconciliation commissions" that valiantly attempt to heal horrific wounds in victimized societies, taking a Christian-influenced approach that calls for confession free of consequences and confers forgiveness and reconciliation, but misses the hard work: the middle step of justice through compensation. Without real justice, perpetrators are prematurely absolved of responsibility, vengeance is allowed to fester, and the toxicity of violence is not taken to heart. Here is the Talmud's teaching:

> Whoever angers his friend, even in words, must reconcile with him ... Rav Hisda says: he must reconcile with him with three sets of three people ... Rabbi Yosi bar Hanina says: whoever seeks forgiveness from his friend should not seek it from him more than three times ... Rabbi Zera, when he had an issue with someone, would pass back and forth before him and make himself available to him, so that he would come and settle the matter. (Talmud, Yoma 87a)

According to Jewish law, it is the responsibility of the injuring party to pursue the hard work of reconciliation, not only for physical and financial injuries which require monetary compensation, but even for verbal and emotional injuries, which require sincere apology. Even so, there are limits set on how far the injuring party needs to go to earn forgiveness, and the victim is enjoined to be tractable, and even to help facilitate the process proactively.[31] Even though forgiveness and reconciliation are ideals, the human condition requires that they be approached with delicacy, patience and forbearance.[32] The Jewish approach to apology and forgiveness asks both the injuring and injured parties, joined in underlying mutual love and unconditional mutual respect, to grow in sensitivity and responsibility through the process.

The Jewish approach to forgiveness is not limited to inter-personal relations but also refers to broader collective purposes.

A collective, large-scale example of a reconciliation process attuned to Jewish sensibilities is the gradual, multi-dimensional, painstaking and painful process of cautious reconciliation that has been ongoing between the Jewish and German peoples after the Holocaust. While reconciliation between first generation Jewish survivors and Nazi perpetrators has generally not been possible, their descendants have been engaged in a second-degree process that has occasionally featured responsible attempts to offer sincere apology and serious efforts at compensatory justice, however hopelessly inadequate, and a deeply thoughtful consideration of how apology can possibly be received for crimes of such magnitude. The gradual warming of political relations between the nations of Israel and Germany is at least a surface indicator, however limited, of the hard work of real healing that has been going on for decades between these two communities, though much work remains to be done. For Israelis and Palestinians, on the other hand, still engaged in conflict, real reconciliation has not begun. Even if eventually there is sufficient reduction of conflict to allow a process of mutual apology, compensation and forgiveness to gain traction, serious problems will persist. Cultural and religious differences between the parties regarding attitudes to revenge and forgiveness, and differing narratives and identities regarding the roles of victim and victimizer, promise to present profound challenges, the overcoming of which will call forth deep spiritual resources from both sides.[33]

The wisdom of the Jewish approach to love and forgiveness, with its call for a universal love that entails concrete responsibility with exquisite sensitivity and respect for the individual, may yet have an important contribution to make in helping heal the wounds and address the terrible violence from which our world suffers today.

NOTES

1. 1 Kings 5:9–14.
2. Proverbs 21:30: "There is no wisdom, no understanding and no counsel overagainst the Lord." The prophet Jeremiah distinguishes between wisdom and direct knowledge of God: "Thus says the Lord: let not the wise man praise himself for his wisdom, let not the strong man praise himself for his strength, let not the rich man praise himself for his riches; rather, let he who praises praise himself for this: to intuit and know Me, that I am the Lord, doing love, judgment and righteous in the earth, for these are what I desire, says the Lord (Jer. 9:22,23).
3. Jerusalem Talmud tractate *Makkot* 2:6 (31): "They asked wisdom . . . they asked prophecy . . . they asked the Holy One, blessed be He." Lamentations Rabbah, 2:13. *Sifrei* Deuteronomy, sec. 34 (on Deut. 6:7); *Sifra*, Aharei Mot 13:11 on Lev. 18:4. The term "Greek wisdom" is also used as a specific example of "wisdom of the nations," though this term has other connotations. See G. J. Blidstein, "Rabbinic Judaism and General Culture: Normative Discussion and Attitudes," in *Judaism's Encounter with Other Cultures,* ed. J. J. Schacter (Northvale, NJ and Jerusalem: 1997), 1–56, for a survey of views of the Talmudic period.
4. In the Talmud tractate *Shabbat* 75a, that which is considered wisdom in the eyes of the nations is defined narrowly and concretely, as astronomical calculations for the sake of setting the calendar, or for predicting the weather (Rashi, loc. cit.). This kind of specificity in interpretation is characteristic of talmudic discussions, and is not always to be construed strictly. Rather, the specific identification is in certain instances meant to be exemplary, sometimes for homiletic purposes. Here, the exhortatory thrust of the statement is to encourage Jews to value, cultivate and utilize this socially important skill. The implication is that this is an example of a technical skill set with legal and scientific ramifications, whose value also happens to translate outside a Jewish religious context. Astronomical wisdom of Jews can be admired by non-Jews because it is religiously neutral, involving the objective observation of nature, something that can be shared across religious cultures.
5. Moses Maimonides, *Teshuvot ha-Rambam,* vol. 3, resp. 57. R. Solomon Ibn Adret, *She'elot u-Teshuvot,* vol. 1, resp. 260, 415, 418. R. Menachem ha-Meiri, *Avot,* introduction. See D. Berger, "Judaism and General Culture in Medieval and Early Times," in *Judaism's Encounter with Other Cultures,* ed. J. J. Schacter (Northvale, NJ and Jerusalem: 1997), 57–142, for a survey of Jewish views of the medieval period.
6. *Megillah* 16a: Rabbi Yohanan says: "whoever speaks a word of wisdom, even among the nations of the world, is called a sage."
7. *Hagigah* 13a: Rabbi Ami said, "One does not transmit words of Torah to a non-Jew, as it says "He did not do so for any nation, and of the laws they do not know (Ps. 147:20). "Torah" here refers to the content and methodology of the legal tradition.

8. Deut. 4:5, 6: "Behold I have taught you statutes and laws as the Lord my God commanded me, to do accordingly in the midst of the land that you are going to, to inherit. Observe them and do them, for it is your wisdom and understanding in the eyes of the nations, who will hear all these statutes and say: surely a wise and understanding people is this great nation." Medieval commentators such as Rashi and R. Avraham Ibn Ezra take this passage broadly: that the wisdom of the statutes and laws of the Torah will be apparent to other nations and admired by them. This is because these laws will be perceived to be inherently rational (Ibn Ezra, Commentary on the Torah, *loc. cit.*), or because of their moral and spiritual benefits. In the Talmud tractate *Shabbat* 75a, that which is considered "wisdom and understanding in the eyes of the nations" is defined narrowly, as astronomical calculations. These verses indicate an expectation of communication between Jews and non-Jews on issues of law and religion, and a concern the foster a positive attitude among non-Jewish towards Jews and Jewish wisdom.

9. See, for instance, *Menahot* 99b, regarding the primacy of Torah study that renders study of Greek wisdom superfluous.

10. Maimonides, *Mishneh Torah*, Laws of Kings 12:4, 5 e.

11. See the Mishnah Commentary of R. Jonah Gerondi, *ad loc.*: "Pore over the words of Torah, for all the wisdom of the world is comprised in it." See, also, the commentaries of R. Ovadiah Bertinoro, R. Yom Tov Lippman Heller.

12. Commentary on *Avot*, cited in *Midrash Shmuel*, ad loc.

13. Compare, for precedent, Maimonides, *Mishneh Torah*, Foundations of the Torah 2:1; Laws of Repentance, 10: 6. R. Aharon Lichtenstein discusses this Mishnaic statement at length, and analyzes multiple perspectives on the issue of mutual sharing of wisdom between Jews and non-Jews, in his article "Torah and General Culture: Confluence and Conflict," in *Judaism's Encounter with Other Cultures*, 237–72.

14. *Ketav Hitnazlut*, in *She'elot u-Teshuvot ha-Rashba* (Bnei Brak, 1958) 1:418. See, too, R. Moses Ibn Ezra (c.1055-c.1135), *Shirat Yisrael*, ed. B. Z. Halper (Leipzig: 1924), 63.

15. Maimonides, *Mishne Torah*, Laws of Repentance 10:6. Maimonides expands upon a prior discussion in Laws of Foundations of the Torah 2:1, on the need for scientific and philosophic knowledge to fulfill the commandment to love God. In his time, the "wisdoms and understandings" of which he speaks came from the worldwide matrix of Hellenistic wisdom developed by and shared among the Western religious traditions. Thus Maimonides is saying that shared wisdom is necessary to adequately fulfill one of the most spiritually profound commandments of the Torah: to love God.

16. R. Barukh Schick of Shklov (d. 1808), *Sefer Euklidos*, Introduction. Compare the remarks of R. Samson Rafael Hirsch (1808–1888), "Die judischen Hoffnungen in Ungarn," *Jeschurun* 15 (1869): 20–22, cited in S. Z. Leiman, "Rabbinic Openness to General Culture in the Early Modern Period in Western and Central Europe," *Judaism's Encounter with Other Cultures*, 196–97.

17. R. Abraham Isaac Kook, *Orot* (Jerusalem: 1969), 152.

18. R. Abraham Isaac Kook, *Letters*, vol. 1, letter 112, in *Abraham Isaac Kook*, trans. B. Z Bokser (Mahwah, NJ: 1978), 338–39.

19. Just one example among many: *Berakhot* 8b: "Rabbi Akiva would say, 'for three things I love the Medeans. When they slice meat, they only slice it on a table. When they kiss, they only kiss on the back of the hand. When they offer advice, they only offer advice in an open field.' It is taught that Rabban Gamliel would say, 'for three things I love the Persians. They are modest in their eating, modest in the bathroom, and modest regarding the other matter.'" Rabbi Akiva and Rabban Gamliel demonstrate a knowledge of Medean and Persian culture, and a positive assessment of some of their practical customs regarding hygiene and personal relations.

20. *Pesahim* 94b

21. For instance, *Sanhedrin* 91b features discussions on ensoulment of an embryo between Rabbi Yehudah ha-Nasi, political and intellectual leader of the Jewish community in the Land of Israel, and an Emperor Antoninus, according to some scholarly

opinions the Emperor Marcus Aurelius Antoninus Caracalla, a contemporary of Rabbi Yehudah ha-Nasi, known for his good relations with the Jewish people: See S. Krauss, *Antoninus und Rabbi* (Vienna: 1910), 98.

22. Moses Maimonides, *Mishneh Torah*, Foundations of the Torah 2:10.

23. To take one common example, the terms "form" and "matter" in the Aristotelian sense are found throughout the legal literature of the medieval and modern periods, and in the spiritual literature of Hassidism, even among authors who vigorously reject the study of philosophy. See, e.g. R. Issac Jacob Weiss, *Minhat Yitzhak* 4:17. R. Ovadya Yosef, *Yabia Omer*, vol. 5, O. H. 42. R. Yehudah Aryeh Leib Alter of Gur, *Sefat Emet*, Parshat BeMidbar, 5637.

24. R. David Ibn Abi Zimra, *She'elot u-Tshuvot*, vol. 3 (New York: 1967) resp. 472. Maimonides, *Mishneh Torah*, H. Talmud Torah, 4:1.

25. E. Levinas, *Totality and Infinity*, trans. A. Lingis (Pittsburgh: 1969), 21, 46–47, 127; J. Derrida, *Writing and Difference*, trans. A. Bass (Chicago: 1978), 89.

26. I. Even-Zohar, "Laws of Literary Interference," in *Poetics Today: Polysystem Studies*, vol. 11, no. 1 (Durham, NC: Spring 1990), 53–72. For instance, Jewish thinkers of the eleventh through thirteenth centuries pick up the subtleties of philosophic discussions of attribute theory taking place contemporaneously in Christianity and Islam and find them useful for articulating a theology of monotheism, but show no interest in the subtleties of Christian discussions of trinitarianism taking place at the same time.

27. J. B. Soloveitchik, "A Stranger and a Resident," *Reflections of the Rav*, ed. A. R. Besdin (Hoboken, NJ: 1993), 176–77. The essay was published in 1964. The Second Vatican Council took place from 1962–65.

28. See G. Scholem, "Religious Authority and Mysticism," *On the Kabbalah and Its Symbolism*, trans. R. Manheim (New York: 1970), 5–21, for a seminal discussion of this issue.

29. Maimonides, *Mishneh Torah*, Foundations of the Torah, 1:1–6.

30. See, e.g., the interpretation of R. Barukh Epstein, *Torah Temimah*, vol. 1 (Tel Aviv: 1957), 72, note 2, on Gen. 5:1.

31. Talmud tractate *Yuma* 87a, b. See Maimonides, *Mishneh Torah*, De'ot 7:7, regarding the basis of the prohibition against revenge.

See, too, Maimonides, *Mishneh Torah*, Laws of Repentance, 2:10:

> It is forbidden for a person to be cruel and not be appeased, rather, he should be easy to satisfy and hard to get angry, and when a sinner asks him to forgive him he should forgive with a whole heart and a willing soul. Even if he afflicted him and sinned against him greatly, he should not be vengeful and bear a grudge. This is the way of the seed of Israel and their health of heart.

32. *Yuma* 87 a, b. See E. Levinas, *Nine Talmudic Readings*, trans. A. Aronowicz (Bloomington, IN: 1994), 12–25, for an in-depth phenomenological analysis of this passage.

33. See D. Bar-On, "Will the Parties Conciliate or Refuse? The Triangle of Jews, Germans and Palestinians," *From Conflict Resolution to Reconciliation*, ed. Y. Bar-Siman-Tov (Oxford: 2004), 239–52.

SEVEN

Sharing Wisdom

A Composite Picture

Alon Goshen-Gottstein

FINDING A COMMON VOICE

My purpose in the present chapter is not to summarize or repeat what the individual chapters have suggested. Rather, I would like to pull together various insights and key notions found in the individual chapters and to draw a composite picture of the subject. As a composite picture, it seeks to draw on the presentations of all the chapters, attempting to find the commonalities, without flattening the differences between the individual traditions. Of course, the synthesis is my own personal attempt at offering an overview of the project. As such it must suffer from my own biases, primary among which is my theistic approach to issues (to which a Buddhist could take exception) and possibly my own Jewish orientation as well. I therefore offer the following synthesis as a personal statement, rather than as a consensus reached by our group of scholars. I note with satisfaction that this synthesis is close in spirit to the common voice expressed in the book's introduction as a statement of consensus.

Perhaps the place to begin tackling the challenge of drawing together the different perspectives expressed in the chapters with a recognition of significant differences in the very approach to sharing wisdom. Different religions seem to approach the subject in different ways, and with differing degrees of comfort and openness. While all our scholars have successfully engaged the topic and pointed the way forward from the perspective of their tradition, there seem to be different levels of comfort with the notion of sharing wisdom, different degrees of concern in relation to the risks and dangers involved in sharing wisdom and different degrees of calling for care and caution. Thus, judging by the tone, as well as the content, of the chapters, the Jewish and Buddhist perspectives seem to be on opposite sides of the spectrum, with Judaism exhibiting the greatest degree of concern and care in relation to our project, while Buddhism and its notion of the use of skillful means to adapt the core teaching to changing circumstances has the easiest time relating to our project. Islam seems to exhibit concerns similar to those of Judaism, which stands to reason, given the common starting point of a religion based on revealing divine wisdom through Scripture. Sikhism and Christianity both seem to consider sharing wisdom a natural expression of their religious life. It is thus appropriate to acknowledge important differences in nuance between the chapters. These differences may stem from differing understandings of wisdom and consequently of the possibility of sharing it. My own synthesis is mindful of these differences, even as it seeks to uncover the deeper commonalities that I see emerging from the multiple voices.

SHARING WISDOM—BETWEEN THE UNIVERSAL AND THE PARTICULAR

As Miroslav Volf astutely points out, sharing wisdom assumes similarity as well as dissimilarity.[1] It assumes a single humanity living in one world. At the same time, this single humanity is differentiated, and it is this diversity that creates the specific need for sharing wisdom. Diversity is not total otherness. It is because we are both alike and different that we seek to share wisdom across religious dividing lines. Thus, the sharing of wisdom is a bridge between two fundamental dimensions that characterize all our religions—the universal and the particular. For wisdom to be recognized as such it must have an appeal beyond the teachings of a particular tradition. Wisdom is by its essence, as well as following historical precedent, a universal phenomenon.[2] And yet, each tradition, and consequently its wisdom, is couched within a particularity, be it national, cultural, sociological or other. It is worth acknowledging that even while affirming a single world and a single humanity, one can conceive of multiple wisdoms. Thus, in the case of Islam, while humanity is one, its constituents are many, and each is entrusted with a different aspect of wisdom, along with the command to learn from one another.[3] Sharing is thus constructing a bridge between the universal and the particular.

It is worth noting that both the unity of the world and the unity of mankind are highlighted in all our chapters. In fact it is this unity of the world and the unity of humanity that provide the impetus for sharing wisdom, for some of our authors.[4]

Wisdom can help us navigate the tension between the particular and the universal as we consider the relationship of wisdom and God. It is very helpful to note, in this context, the Muslim position, according to which God's wisdom, which emanates from the "mother book," far exceeds his revelation.[5] We actually find similar statements in Rabbinic literature, according to which the Torah is but a pale reflection of the supernal wisdom.[6] True wisdom is thus, as the Sikhs teach us, the attainment of the divine and its attributes.[7] While it goes without saying that such a formulation remains beyond the pale of what a Buddhist could subscribe to, this formulation could serve as a common denominator for all theistic traditions, offering us the ultimate yardstick by means of which to measure traditions, their evolution and the degree to which they are effective carriers of true wisdom. True wisdom always points beyond the particular form of religious expression to the ultimate source of all religious traditions—God Himself. Thus, to speak of wisdom, and more specifically of divine wisdom, provides us with a way of bridging the universal and the particular. Wisdom is that which is universal and which manifests in the particular. It is that which prevents our individual traditions from closing in on themselves and keeps them open to the broader divine vision, the wisdom that both precedes religions and is grounded in them.[8]

Several authors have touched upon the relations of sharing wisdom and peacemaking.[9] Sharing wisdom is related to peacemaking in obvious ways. It allows us to remove the misunderstandings that harbor enmity and lead to violent behavior. In light of the attempt to consider wisdom's role as the bridge between the universal and the particular we may gain a deeper insight into the relationship between the sharing of wisdom and making peace. Most situations in which violence is manifest are situations in which the particular rules and sight has been lost of the universal. In the case of religious violence, it is only possible when complete identification with the particular takes place, to the exclusion of recognition of other manifestations of the universal. The quest for wisdom is by definition a quest for the universal and for the dynamic relations between the particular and the universal, within one's own tradition, as well as within other traditions. It is thus a quest that takes us away from complete identification with the particular form of our traditions and into the search for the higher divine wisdom and purpose. The movement towards the universal is a movement towards peace. Seeking wisdom is, ultimately, seeking peace.

A different way of stating the same thing would be to consider the tension, or movement, between human wisdom and divine wisdom. To the degree we identify wisdom and God, then by wisdom we really mean divine wisdom. Yet, our traditions are full of the activities of sages. Some of these sages consciously seek divine wisdom, others don't, even as some of our traditions can speak of wisdom without associating it with the divine. An examination of the chapters shows that while some of our authors focused upon divine wisdom, others approached wisdom in relation to human sages.[10] I believe it is fair to say that each of our traditions has forms or precedents that highlight the human component of wisdom and those that seek the divine, or the metaphysical reality as it is in and of itself. Wisdom is thus elusive. It is both the primary reality, manifesting itself through the human reality,[11] and that human reality itself. This tension around the question of who is the actor, or whose wisdom is made manifest, is what situates wisdom between the universal and the particular. Timothy Gianotti and Pal Ahluwalia both point to the relation between wisdom and other divine attributes.[12] Attributes are what humans share with the divine. Attributes can thus be variously manifested as more or less human, more or less divine. Wisdom is thus the common bridge between the human and the divine, the particular and the universal.

Wisdom can, accordingly, also be the goal of the common quest that unites practitioners of different religions. Timothy Gianotti has suggested that rather than thinking of ourselves as sharing "our" wisdom with others, we should conceive of ourselves as engaged in the common quest for wisdom.[13] The realization that wisdom provides the bridge from the human to the divine and from the particular to the universal makes this formulation particularly appealing. As we are all placed upon the axis between the human and the divine, or that of moving from human limitations to transcending them, the quest for wisdom is a common human quest. Gianotti's call simply articulates a reality that we have all been living for thousands of years. We have all been seeking wisdom ever since our religions have come into being. Now, suggests Gianotti, is the time for us to do so together.

Situating wisdom between the universal and the particular allows us to explore different forms of sharing wisdom and their respective benefits. Within wisdom's range, what aspect do we seek to share? Is sharing an attempt to uncover the common, universal core, that may underlie all traditions, or is it the attempt to share the unique, particular, perhaps even strange? Is the wisdom that can be seen by others as folly,[14] also part of the wisdom we seek to share, or should the sharing of wisdom be limited to those forms of wisdom already recognized as such by practitioners of other faiths.

It is important to pay careful attention to the various strategies by means of which the teaching of the other is legitimated in terms of wisdom. The easiest, and most comprehensive, strategy is the apophatic strategy used by Rambachan and Ahluwalia. According to this strategy, all our speech, thought and understanding of God are limited, inferior and unable to capture the divine in and of itself. The response to the limitations of our understanding is the recognition of how partial is the teaching of all traditions, in face of the absolute.[15] This could, in theory, lead to a dismissal of all attempts to articulate religious understanding as invalid or as of limited significance, and hence undeserving of our attention.[16] In Rambachan's hands, voicing the Hindu tradition, this creates an openness to all traditions as potential carriers of valid insight concerning the divine. Rambachan goes as far as to suggest that this key insight can be exported from Hinduism to other traditions.[17] A different way of putting this might be that an apophatic strain may be found in every tradition. All that remains is for us to engage in a reflection on the meaning of "negative theology," as it is often called, to interreligious relations.

While this is a powerful strategy for recognizing the other and opening up to the wisdom of another tradition, we also encounter in our essays strategies based on the positive action of God, rather than the negative limitations of human understanding. These strategies may be presented as different forms of the gift theory. According to this theory, wisdom is the gift of God, and He has given it in various contexts. These contexts are broader than the boundaries of individual religious traditions and this allows members of those individual traditions to recognize wisdom beyond their own tradition.[18] The Muslim understanding according to which God's signs are everywhere and that God has given each community something valuable to share with the other is a form of such a theory.[19] Rav Kook's theory of the spreading of aptitudes among the nations, leading to symbiotic and peaceful relations, is another form of a gift theory.[20]

Both the gift theory and the apophatic approach[21] address the intricacies of the relations of the universal and the particular. Both attempt to account for the particular in light of the universal and to legitimate difference and particularity. Wisdom is clearly universal and as such is captured in some way by all our traditions. But it is also particular and as such invites us to the sharing of that wisdom in its very particularity. That particularity may be validated in terms of the human reality and our need to come to understand it, in the interests of peace. But it may also be validated in terms of the divine reality, as it expresses itself in and through the particular. Here we open up to the possibility that sharing wisdom, in its particularity, is a sharing of divine wisdom, or at the very least, an expression of a common quest for divine wisdom, that cuts across religious traditions.

THE CONCERN FOR AUTHENTICITY AND INTEGRITY

While sharing wisdom holds much promise, it is also a project that must be approached with care. Approached with care, it can yield meaningful and transformative fruit for religions and for society. Lacking the needed caution, it can have undesired effects. In considering the concerns that this project raises, one may sum them up in terms of authenticity and integrity. Sharing wisdom must respect the integrity of the overall structure from which the wisdom is shared, as it is extracted and offered in a new context, a new translation. As wisdom is shared in today's world, it often takes pieces of advice out of their context, thereby losing the integrity of the whole, of the totality that is itself a sign and an expression of wisdom. To the extent that sharing wisdom is a means of offering life support when systems of meaning collapse, perhaps we need not be unduly concerned with the purity of the teaching and its integrity. When we face the individual in crisis we seek to heal that individual, and any medicine that comes to hand may be used. But sharing wisdom is more than offering the first available remedy to a person in distress. Sharing wisdom is also a strategy for bringing communities together, for addressing global ills and for growth and transformation of individuals as well as broader religious systems. It is here that greater care must be applied.

Miroslav Volf has spelled out some of the problems with extracting pieces of wisdom, nuggets of wisdom as he calls them, from their context and inserting them into new structures of meaning.[22] Totality and wholeness are essential to the wisdom of the way of life that religion offers. Striking at that very totality is a way of undermining the integrity, hence the wisdom, of the specific religious way. This is a struggle that all our religions face. On the one hand we are always on the lookout for new ways in which to offer our teachings to our audiences, both old and new. On the other hand, the new forms of teaching must respect the coherence of the totality of the way of life. This is a struggle already within each of our religions. Sharing wisdom between members of different religions heightens the tensions further.

These issues are particularly relevant to the cause of wisdom because, as Anant Rambachan makes us aware, wisdom is itself founded upon integration. Wisdom is an integrated mode of being.[23] While the details of how such integration is conceived of may change from religion to religion, I believe it is fair to say that all our traditions would establish a close relationship between wisdom and integration—the integration of heart and mind, thought and action, individual and community, body and spirit. What threatens our traditions, as suggested in an earlier volume in this series, devoted to "The Crisis of the Holy," is the breakdown of this integrity and the loss of comprehensiveness of meaning that religion seeks to offer.[24] The wisdom of religious traditions is appreciated precisely as a testimony to the wholeness of life. The sharing of wisdom must thus find the middle path between the desire to extend wisdom beyond its original home and the need to preserve that very sense of wholeness and integrity that allow us to recognize it as wisdom in the first instance.

The issue arises, to a large extent, because the context for sharing wisdom has changed. Rambachan has highlighted the classical context of teacher-disciple relations within which the sharing of wisdom has classically taken place.[25] The point has come up in just about all the papers in one way or another. Today the imparting of wisdom takes place in a much broader context, both within each religion and beyond it. This new context also offers new ways of conceiving or reconfiguring the meaning of totality. Timothy Gianotti suggests that outside of the teacher-student paradigm and in the context of the sharing of wisdom between religions, we ought to think of how wisdom is mutually sought, pondered and cherished by believers of multiple faith traditions.[26] Their sincerity and the unifying intention of seeking with open minds and hearts provide an alternative to the integrity of the original context of acquiring wisdom. Thus, the common quest is, for Gianotti, a new context that almost redefines the meaning of integrity and authenticity. Purity of mind and heart are what protect the common quest from some of the pitfalls that contemporary sharing of wisdom suffers from. Thus, integrity is reconstituted.

A second meaningful insight comes up in several of the papers. Sallie King mentions what an example Gandhi was for the Dalai Lama.[27] Rambachan offers us a theory, supported with some moving quotes from Vivekananda, of how inspiration and example can and should be carried over beyond the boundaries of traditions.[28] The example of the individual teacher or saint remains a powerful means of educating and hence of sharing wisdom. Even if traditional teacher-student relations have undergone transformation, and perhaps even broken down, the power of personal example as a source of inspiration endures. And it endures in a world in which that personal example radiates to ever broader circles, reaching beyond the limits of the spiritual tradition that provided the inspiration for the personal example. Personal example and the enactment of wisdom in concrete life situations may be even more powerful in a media-conscious culture that amplifies the individual person and the individual deed, elevating them in public consciousness. Thus, sharing wisdom is achieved through the lived teaching of the individual, the example of the believer, the practitioner, the teacher, the saint.

In this context it is worth reflecting upon the challenges of sharing wisdom in relation to the subject of the previous volume in our series — religious leadership.[29] The first beneficiaries of these chapters were members of the Elijah Board of World Religious Leaders. In a meaningful way, not only their faith communities but also those of other communities, the world at large, look to them as models for wisdom in action, offering their testimony and example to the world at large. Perhaps one significant way of sharing wisdom in the context of bringing together religious leaders to engage this topic is the raising of awareness of how global the need is for role models and personal examples of lived wisdom. The challenge of religious leadership today extends beyond the classical confines of our tradition, just as the spreading of wisdom extends beyond the parameters of teacher-student relations.

The problem of authenticity has other significant expressions as well. These are highlighted in the clearest way in the presentation of the Jewish view of sharing wisdom. The concern for authenticity informs Sendor's entire presentation. Protection of the authentic teaching and approach to the Divine constitutes the core narrative of Judaism's sharing wisdom with other religions. The more one emphasizes teaching, a natural by-product of revelation and the scriptures that are born of it, the more the concern for authenticity increases. Sendor is accordingly concerned about inauthentic syncretism and generalization and the obscuring of important distinctions between the faiths.[30] We note the choice of "inauthentic" to designate erroneous teaching or understanding. Misunderstanding is perhaps the greatest enemy and while the drive for sharing is upheld, Sendor provides us with a battery of precautions, all of which are meant to safeguard the authenticity of teaching.

The process of sharing wisdom must confront fundamental obstacles. There is, however, a great distance between the fundamental obstacles to sharing wisdom, based on the difficulty in communicating experience properly, that Sallie King highlights,[31] and the problems of boundaries and their appropriate maintenance, as teaching is protected from misunderstanding. Different as these issues are, and different as their practical consequences in relation to actual sharing of wisdom are,[32] there is one key issue that is common to them. Both express the concern for authenticity. And contemporary society only heightens the tension around authenticity, as the different traditions battle to preserve the integrity of their tradition in the face of multiple external forces.[33]

Discussion of authenticity leads us to consider its relationship to identity. Loss of identity is the biggest fear that sharing wisdom could trigger.[34] Receiving too much from the outside could feel like an unwelcome undoing of one's very self. The history of Jewish wisdom sharing, as told by Sendor, provides an example of the concern and the struggle for maintaining the sense of Self.[35] Perhaps it is no accident that Buddhism approaches the problem with so much ease, and perhaps its openness to multiple religious identities is itself related to a lesser concern with maintaining the integrity and identity of the self, given its own approach to issues of self and identity.

However, as vital as the protection of tradition is, we must also consider that none of our traditions exist in a pure state, and that they are all contaminated by the original sin of sharing wisdom. We all enter the quest for preserving the integrity of our religious identity after already having been touched in some way by the other, and having been already transformed by that touch.[36] The way in which Judaism, Christianity and Islam were all transformed through the encounter with each other and with Hellenistic Philosophy is an important instance of sharing wisdom that touches the heart of the religion. One hears Sendor's struggles as he seeks to situate the authentic Jewish understanding of God, viewed through the various stages of its articulation in the history of Jewish thought.[37] But maybe that is something we must give further thought to—is it possible, hundreds and thousands of years later, to speak of a religious tradition in its pure form. The quest for authenticity carries with it dangers. These are manifest in some of the reactionary religious forms that are born of the attempt to recreate a lost authenticity. In a more philosophical vein, there is the danger of undoing the movement of growth a tradition has undergone, a growth which may itself be part of the divine design for its evolution. At the same time, letting go of the quest for authenticity is tantamount to deep betrayal of our own commitment to tradition.

We are thus pulled towards an equilibrium that is hard to articulate. It is an equilibrium that recognizes change, transformation, and, above all, the influence that comes from sharing on the one hand, while upholding a sense of identity, commitment and authenticity, on the other. The dynamics of this equilibrium may be hard to describe, especially as they vary from one tradition to the other and from one historical manifestation to another. It is this very equilibrium that allows us to engage in sharing wisdom while at the same time maintaining our sense of religious authenticity and identity. It is this equilibrium that allows us to uphold the age-old teachings of our tradition even as we seek new ways to give them expression. The difficulty is that an equilibrium is not a fixed set of rules. It is an internal guide, a spiritual code, in a word—a particular expression of wisdom. And it is as elusive as wisdom itself. Different people, different religions and different streams within them, may grasp this equilibrium differently. It remains a source of contention, even of conflict. And yet, it also carries with it the traces of the wisdom that could allow us to recognize when the balance of authenticity and growth is appropriate and when it is not.

A suggestive idea comes to mind. Our different traditions, while all partaking of the primordial sin of sharing wisdom, offer different theories in relation to the sharing of wisdom. When viewed in their entirety could they not suggest an equilibrium that is worthy of consideration? As we focus our attention on the dynamics of identity, change and influence as expressed within the totality of our traditions, we recognize the same forces we encounter, in most cases, within the individual traditions. Accordingly, there is wisdom in noting our differences, because they are complementary and they could provide the elements of the full equilibrium required for appropriate sharing of wisdom between religious traditions. It is important to hear the Buddhist voice encouraging borrowing of techniques and respecting multiple religious identities even as it is important to hear the Jewish voice that calls for care and concern, lest error settle into the teaching of our religions. It is important to note how the dynamics of acculturation and translation have affected Christianity, even as we note that Hindu teaching, as well as Sikh teaching, continue to draw on classical master-disciple relations and the demands of discipline and the spiritual life that accompany them. Sharing the wisdom of how we share wisdom may provide us with the wisdom to share wisdom. That is: each of our traditions, as expressed in our chapters, emphasizes a different aspect of a complex dynamic in relation to sharing wisdom. The complexity of wisdom leads us to recognize the need for integrating some aspect of each of these approaches. We thus need to learn from others how they share wisdom, what their dynamics and concerns are. This opens for us a window to a better understanding of what wisdom is, and enriches how we seek and disseminate wisdom. The combined wisdom of our traditions may present an equilibrium that is itself an expression of the higher wisdom, in which all our traditions are rooted.

SHARING WISDOM AND MISSION

A discussion of authenticity leads us to a consideration of the relationship of sharing wisdom and missionary activity. Sharing wisdom could be viewed with suspicion as a strategy for proselytization. The strong impetus that exists in some of our religions to share their wisdom, truth and faith with others raises the need to distinguish between sharing wisdom and missionizing. I would like to suggest that fuller awareness of the conditions for appropriate sharing could actually provide a direction in handling the thorny issue of conversion and mission.

Sharing wisdom is founded upon reciprocity. Even if it does not assume full equality and does not partake of a relativistic view of religious teaching in relation to the ultimate truth, it nevertheless does assume the possibility of meaningful sharing in a reciprocal movement, which is based on some degree of mutual recognition. In this sense, sharing wisdom is opposed to missionary activity, that usually ignores the inherent value of the other, or trivializes it to the point of attempting to supplant it by means of an alternative religious identity. The attitude of responsible sharing of wisdom thus provides an alternative, and hence a way of addressing an issue that causes great concern in India, in the Jewish community and elsewhere. Sharing wisdom opens us up to a broader range of understandings of both what wisdom is and how to share it wisely. When more than one view of these issues is acknowledged, we will have broken beyond the narrower view of inter-group relations, associated with efforts at proselytization.

The recognition that all religions have something important to say to the human person does not preclude the possibility that the appeal of wisdom might lead a person to adopt a new way of religious life. However, the process leading up to such a decision would be completely different. It would be based on the recognition of multiple wisdom traditions, rather than one that overrides all others. It would be based on offering testimony and witness, rather than on any of a number of coercive and disrespectful methods that are often employed in missionary activities.[38] Perhaps most importantly, true sharing of wisdom is not associated with ego and considerations of personal and group identity, that often accompany proselytization. As Volf points out, wisdom is the primary reality, and it seeks to impart itself.[39] Letting wisdom impart itself leads to the removal of the individual ego. In true sharing of wisdom it is wisdom that is active, not the excited believer.

THE COMMERCIALIZATION OF WISDOM

As noted in the introduction, the present project was born from a challenge posed by Sri Sri Ravi Sankar concerning the possibility of sharing wisdom in an increasingly globalized world. Underlying Sri Sri's question is a marketplace reality in which goods travel and are exchanged and in which wisdom itself is commodified and shared. This reality, much like globalization itself, has positive as well as negative aspects. Its positive aspects are the accessibility of knowledge and the ease of its dissemination. These allow for an open-ended invitation to share wisdom, as part of a process of spiritual growth, that all religions can jointly contribute to.

But inspiring as this vision may be, there is also a flip side to it. The wisdom of our traditions is a wisdom of wholeness. This wholeness cannot be adequately expressed in the marketplace. The very process of commodification of wisdom alters something fundamental about it, as it extracts it from its context of wholeness. The problem of "nuggetization" that our chapters deal with grapples with this issue: how to relate to the nuggets of wisdom taken out of the totality of tradition and shared with others, mainly in a commercial or semi-commercial context. Resisting the commodification and commercialization of wisdom seem to be one of the strongest points of agreement between scholars involved in the present project.[40] The identification of wisdom with God is Gianotti's way of ensuring that wisdom is not commodified.[41] This would mean that the quest for wisdom must remain mindful of that aspect of transcendent wisdom that is God Himself that continues to inform the wisdom we are able to attain, and that always remains beyond it. Sendor reminds us that the matrix of student-master relationships is designed to offer protection against the commodification of wisdom.[42] Miroslav Volf states clearly that wisdom is betrayed when it is bought and sold.[43] The commodification and commercialization of wisdom place a score of temptations on the path of the seeker of wisdom. These include tailoring wisdom to the desire of its potential buyers, the distortion of wisdom and the possibility of taking advantage of the potential seeker. Commercialization allows the buyer to pick and choose as much or as little of the wisdom as suits them.

Wisdom then no longer shapes people's lives, but simply satisfies a desire, or at best addresses a human crisis situation. Thus, the commercialization of wisdom runs the risk of wisdom no longer being the primary reality. Instead, the individual endowed with buying power becomes primary.

It is not simply that those who hold wisdom dear must resist its commercialization. Wisdom could actually provide an antidote to globalizing tendencies that shape our consciousness in commercial terms. All religious communities are under the assault of these tendencies. Some of the violent reactions within specific religious traditions are, at least in part, a reaction to these globalizing tendencies, that are seen as secular and catering to the personal satisfaction of the individual. Wisdom offers a response to these tendencies. It invites us to transcend ourselves in seeking a higher coherence and wholeness. One concrete way of transcending ourselves and our communities in the quest for wisdom informs this project—the sharing of wisdom between different religious traditions.

SHARING WISDOM AND POWER RELATIONS

Both proselytization and commercialization involve us in some way in power relations. It is therefore wise to consider the fact that sharing wisdom does not always happen on a neutral playing ground, in which all parties are equally empowered. Whereas the ideal precondition for healthy sharing of wisdom would be the reciprocal sharing of wisdom by parties that enjoy full parity with one another, the reality is often different. This is, Gianotti reminds us, why interfaith relations are often suspect.[44] The fear that this is one additional expression of imbalances in the distribution of power and wealth cannot be overlooked, as we reflect upon the challenges facing a healthy sharing of wisdom.

The mechanism of receiving and giving wisdom is also affected by how an individual community is situated in the matrix of power relations in relation to broader society. Meir Sendor's presentation makes that point clearly.[45] Being a minority within a host culture conditions the processes of sharing wisdom in Jewish history. One may argue that the sharing of wisdom can never be fully separated from issues of power relations in the political and social order. At the same time, the sharing of wisdom could create an alternative reality that could provide a corrective to power imbalances in the "real" world. When properly executed, the sharing of wisdom is founded upon mutual recognition, meeting at least the minimum requirement of recognizing that the other has something of worth to teach one. Thus, sharing wisdom is related to recognition, which, in turn is related to power relations. In a meaningful way the field of wisdom can make up for conditions prevailing in the social and political order. At the same time, it can never be fully divorced from that order.

What all this means is that awareness and sensitivity are required as we share wisdom. The sharing of wisdom can be a strategy for addressing some of the world's burning issues. But it can only be effective if those very issues are born in mind. Awareness of imbalances in power relations must accompany our exchange of wisdom. Only then can the exchange of wisdom help address those very imbalances.

HUMILITY AND THE SHARING OF WISDOM

In seeking to identify the points of commonality that emerge from the different presentations, one is struck by how humility features in the different presentations as a precondition for sharing wisdom. Despite differences in metaphysics, when it comes to the field of ethics and spirituality, all traditions seem to recognize the importance of humility. Several of the authors have referred to epistemological humility.[46] The ultimate wisdom cannot be known and always remains beyond our grasp. Hence, the attitude to all other traditions must be informed by the humility that is born of our recognition of our own limitations. There are various consequences to this epistemological humility. As wisdom cannot be stated adequately anyway, this allowed the Buddha to adjust his teachings in relation to the capacity of his audience to understand him.[47] Thus, accommodation of the teaching may be the consequence of humility. The limitations of language and understanding also provide the roots for acceptance of the other. Thus, epistemological humility provides a basis for interreligious pluralism.[48]

Despite the appeal of the argument from epistemological humility, we may do well to extract humility from its philosophical implications and to concentrate upon its spiritual virtues and its contribution to interpersonal and inter-group relations. As noted already, while all traditions have an apophatic dimension, there is something unsettling in constructing bridges of understanding between people on the foundation of lack of full or sufficient understanding of God. Even if it is true, it is counterintuitive to traditions whose starting point is the positive knowledge offered by revelation. The argument should actually run that the fuller the knowledge of God, the greater the humility. Knowledge is a part of the complex of attributes that the seeker perfects, as he or she draws closer to God and grows to increasingly resemble Him.[49] Thus, as God supports, sustains and accepts all in His humility, so ought those who grow closer to him. Closeness to God should result in a fuller vision of the divine economy, in which there is room for all.[50] Humility could thus be marshalled as a spiritual and moral virtue leading to making room for others, rather than as the point at which human understanding reaches its inevitable limits, forcing us to accept all others, as a consequence of human limitation.

Closely related to humility is the overcoming of the ego in the process of acquiring wisdom. Ahluwalia has made explicit a spiritual fact found in all our traditions.[51] Ego is the greatest obstacle to gaining wisdom. Now, this is a fact that all traditions uphold. However, it is rare to see a recognition that individual and group ego can easily creep into the relations between groups. Thus, we often encounter the paradox of people who cultivate humility in the context of their own tradition, who cultivate the very opposite in relation to others. Clearly, genuine humility must extend to all arenas. Overcoming ego and its consequences is thus a fundamental need of the spiritual life and it has real and immediate consequences to the project of sharing wisdom. Not only does sharing wisdom require putting aside the ego in an act of listening to the other and learning from her. Sharing wisdom may even be presented as a kind of spiritual exercise, by means of which one can be taken beyond one's limitations and opened up to a higher wisdom. The opening is as much a consequence of what is learned as the attitudinal change, whereby the ego is placed aside, in the act of genuine listening. Seen in this light, sharing wisdom is not simply a remedy to issues in contemporary society and in particular to inter-group relations. Sharing wisdom can actually be an integral part of a core spiritual process, recognized by all our traditions—overcoming the ego, and the liberation and transformation that ensue.

LOVE AND THE SHARING OF WISDOM

Humility is not the only spiritual quality that our authors make repeated appeal to.[52] One also notices the centrality of love to many of the discussions. There is of course a close relationship between love and the overcoming of ego. If wisdom is what takes us beyond our own self-involvement, then love would be its natural expression. Unselfishness and wisdom are related, and the recognition of truth is understood as leading to altruism. For the Hindu and Sikh traditions this is because true wisdom is rooted in the recognition of the unity of all being.[53] The consequences of this recognition are altruism and love of all.

Even without this metaphysical understanding, we can recognize that love, selflessness and compassion are the spiritual high-points that our traditions seek to cultivate.[54] The philosophical, theological and metaphysical reasoning may differ, but the spiritual goal seems closely related—transcending the limitations of the self and growing in love. If Hinduism relies on the fundamental insight of the nature of reality, Christianity relies heavily on the person who is the way and who is love. The details may vary; the fundamental spiritual process seems to be one.

If the movement of the spiritual life is indeed growing from the limitations of the individual to ever broader love, wisdom does indeed have an important role to play in this process. Wisdom paves the way and points our understanding towards the goal. Or from another angle: wisdom is the goal, in light of which our orientation and attitude changes, leading to increased love. And finally: love provides the drive for sharing wisdom. Let us dwell for a moment upon this aspect of their relationship. Some of our papers state explicitly that the driving force behind the sharing of wisdom is love.[55] Both love of God and love of the other are recognized as driving the process of sharing wisdom. The distribution of wisdom among nations, says Rav Kook, is intended to lead to a loving sharing between them.[56] Love is the driver for sharing wisdom.

Love and wisdom are closely related. Wisdom leads to love and love leads to the sharing of wisdom. Seen in the context of transcending ego and self-centerdness, these words take on a completely different meaning than we might ascribe to them otherwise. The love that leads to sharing wisdom must be founded upon transcending the self and its limitations. Herein is the answer and the corrective to much that has gone wrong in the history of sharing wisdom and to many of the pitfalls that we seek to avoid. The test of love is in its selflessness. True love could not bolster individual or group ego. It is a movement of service and care, not of self-aggrandizement. By definition it makes room for the other, which in turn opens up the reciprocal movement of sharing wisdom. This is very different from the one-sided sharing that has been practiced at times and that remains a threat to effective sharing of wisdom. The key is thus selfless love, making room for the other, but above all making room for wisdom itself to reveal itself. We are at most wisdom's instruments. As we grow in humility and love we become better instruments. As we become finer instruments, we are able to share more fully and with greater purity of intention. As our sharing is purified, wisdom and love increase. In this we all come together.

NOTES

1. Volf, 4ff.
2. The universality of wisdom is a hallmark of biblical wisdom, that draws upon a universal wisdom tradition, common to the entire ancient near east. Hellenistic philosophy provides a later universal form of wisdom that serves as a backdrop for various articulations of Judaism, Christianity and Islam, as the chapters of our think tank indicate.
3. See Gianotti, 70–71.
4. Volf, 5. This unity is also the key to finding wisdom in traditions outside Christianity, inasmuch as all things exist in Christ, and hence in Wisdom. See Volf, 11. See also Rambachan, 20; Ahluwalia, 38ff; Sendor, 90. It is noteworthy that Sendor draws the ethical consequences of God's unity in relation to the other in terms of love and forgiveness, but is not explicit about the implications for sharing wisdom. It is this very sense of unity that informs some of the other presentations, leading them to recognize how vital sharing wisdom is and how it is metaphysically grounded. In theory, a Jewish presentation of the theme could have proceeded along similar lines.

Sendor's care for integrity and identity, to be discussed below, led him to downplay the idea and its consequences. It is thus significant that despite the more protective strategy his paper takes, he too articulates the basis of metaphysial unity.

5. Gianotti, 68.

6. See Genesis Rabba 17, 5. Sendor does not discuss directly the question of God and wisdom, because of the specific focus and concern of his paper. Therefore, this dimension, which is present in all the other chapters, with the obvious exception of Buddhism, is absent in his presentation. It is, nevertheless, an important aspect of Jewish reflection on wisdom.

7. See Ahluwalia, 36. See also Gianotti, 62.

8. Several papers touch upon the relationship of wisdom and truth. See Volf, 3; Sendor, 80; Gianotti, 67; and King, 45. Often, one considers truth as the arena of clash between competing religious worldviews. However, reframing truth in terms of wisdom and the recognition that wisdom itself is multi-dimensional could help in mitigating the potential clash of competing truth claims. To the degree these draw upon a prior, or broader, notion of wisdom and to the extent that some of the dimensions of wisdom provide a high-ground for spiritual meeting. The dual insights, concerning wisdom's relation to God and concerning wisdom's place in creation, would cover all religions and their teachings, and allow us to make wisdom, in its divine or cosmic sense, the goal of our quest, rather than truth, conceived exclusively in terms of a particular community, revelation or path.

9. See King, 47. The idea is also implicit in Sendor, 84 and Volf, 6.

10. Notable in this respect are Sendor's treatement of wisdom in Judaism that very much highlights human wisdom in relation to divine revelation, and King, whose metaphysics preclude the identification of Wisdom and the Divine. Wisdom is thus the process of attaining the appropriate or best understanding of reality and drawing the appropriate conclusions.

11. See Volf, 9.

12. See Gianotti, 62ff; Ahluwalia, 36.

13. Gianotti, 73.

14. See Volf, 9.

15. See Rambachan, 21.

16. Some Jewish theories of revelation have resorted to just such a tactic to highlight the superiority of revelation to the partial and imperfect spiritual understanding born of the human attempt to grasp the Divine. R. Yehuda Halevy's views in his *Kuzari* are famous, in this regard.

17. 27.

18. A further extension of the gift theory informs Miroslav Volf's presentation. Wisdom is not only God's gift to us. Gift making is also what we do when we share wisdom with one another.

19. See Gianotti, 68ff.

20. See Sendor, 84ff. While King does not articulate a theoretical basis for the willingness of Buddhists to learn from others (see 47ff), the fact could be accounted for on the basis of a gift theory, provided we consider the gift to be a sharing of aptitudes within the human family, without placing the accent on the prior divine distribution of those gifts.

21. In reading the chapters, one wonders to what extent the Eastern traditions tend more readily to an apophatic approach, and draw its relativising consequences in relation to all religious systems, while the revelation based Abrahamic faiths will feel more comfortable with some kind of gift-based understanding of revelation and wisdom. Full apophaticism would undermine the revelational basis of their religions. As a consequence of this difference, the revelation-based traditions struggle to articulate a meaningful distinction between the essence of wisdom, which is seen to be internal and derives from revelation, and that which can be received from the outside. See Volf, 11; Sendor's note on the text on 84. It is worth nothing that even though Islam is constructed on similar theological premises as Judaism, Gianotti's presentation high-

lights equality in the sharing of wisdom, rather than a core wisdom that selectively receives aspects of other wisdoms. See Gianotti, 70–71. This could, of course, simply be a matter of emphasis.

22. Volf, 9.
23. Rambachan, 20.
24. *The Crisis of the Holy: Challenges and Transformations in World Religions*, ed. Alon Goshen-Gottstein (Lanham, MD: Lexington Books, 2014), 16.
25. Rambachan, 23.
26. Gianotti, 69.
27. King, 51.
28. See in particular Rambachan, 24.
29. See *The Future of Religious Leadership: World Religions in Conversation*, ed. Alon Goshen-Gottstein (Lanham, MD: Lexington Books, 2016).
30. Sendor, 87.
31. See King, 45.
32. King's and Sendor's presentations are, as already suggested, diametrically opposed as far as the basic attitude to the sharing of wisdom between traditions goes. Contrast the ease of taking and giving teachings from and to other religions in King's chapter with the efforts to protect from any possible misunderstanding in Sendor's. While the differences express deep differences in cultural attitude, they also stem from different definitions of what wisdom is. Starting from experience and starting from the historical content of revelation will yield very different approaches to how wisdom is managed.
33. See King, 54.
34. See Volf, 9.
35. Sendor, 85.
36. See Volf, 10; Sendor, 85ff; King, 48ff.
37. Sendor, 89.
38. On the importance of witness, see Volf, 7ff, and Rambachan, 26.
39. Volf, 5.
40. For examples from the Buddhist context, see King, 48.
41. Gianotti, 73.
42. Sendor, 87.
43. Volf, 7.
44. Gianotti, 72.
45. Sendor, 85ff.
46. This is particularly true of the Eastern traditions.
47. King, 51.
48. See in particular Rambachan, 26ff.
49. See Gianotti, 62ff.
50. I do not consider it an accident that Judaism's greatest man of God in the twentieth century also articulated the beautiful theory of divine economy, making room for all. See Sendor, 83ff.
51. See Ahluwalia, 36ff.
52. Actually, whatever is said in relation to love could be said in relation to any of the virtues, all of which are interrelated and all of which have to do with wisdom. However, the repeated appeal to love in our essays leads me to lift it up as a key point that all our traditions point to.
53. Rambachan, 28ff; Ahluwalia, 35.
54. In relation to Buddhism, see King, 52.
55. See in particular Volf, 5; Ahluwalia, 38. See also King, 46, expressed in terms of compassion.
56. Sendor, 85.

Bibliography

Abe, Masao. "The Impact of Dialogue with Christianity on My Self-Understanding as a Buddhist." *Buddhist-Christian Studies*, 9 (1989).
Abe, Ryuichi and Haskel, Peter, trans. and eds. *Great Fool: Zen Master Ryokan—Poems, Letters, and Other Writings*. Honolulu: University of Hawaii Press, 1996.
Ahluwalia, Jasbir Singh. "Inter-religious Relations Today," in *Interfaith Dialogue: Different Perspectives*, ed. Dharam Singh. Patiala: Punjabi University, 2002.
Al-Ghazālī. *The Ninety-Nine Beautiful Names of God*. Translated and with notes by David B. Burrell and Nazih Daher. Islamic Texts Society, 1992, 1995.
Arvind-Pal, Mandair and Schakle, Christopher. *Teachings of the Sikh Gurus: Selections from the Sikh Scriptures*. London: Routledge, 2005.
Assman, Jan. *Moses the Egyptian*. Cambridge, MA: Harvard University Press, 1998.
Barnes, Michael. *Theology and the Dialogue of Religions*. Cambridge: Cambridge University Press, 2002.
Bhogal, Balbinder S. "Ghostly Disorientations: Translating the Adi Granth as the Guru Granth." *Sikh Formations* 3 (June 2007).
Bodhi, Bhikkhu, ed. *In the Buddha's Words: An Anthology of Discourses from the Pali Canon*. Boston: Wisdom Publications, 2005.
Dalai Lama, His Holiness. *Ethics for the New Millennium*. New York: Riverhead Books, 1999.
Delbanco, Andrew. *The Real American Dream: A Meditation on Hope*. Cambridge, MA: Harvard University Press, 1999.
Eck, Diana. *Encountering God: A Spiritual Journey from Bozeman to Banaras*. Boston: Beacon Press, 1993.
Ford, David F. *Christian Wisdom: Desiring God and Learning in Love*. Cambridge: Cambridge University Press, 2007.
Huyler, Stephen P. *Meeting God: Elements of Hindu Devotion*. New Haven, CT: Yale University Press, 2002.
Ibn al-'Arabī. *The Bezels of Wisdom*. Translated and with an introduction by R. W. J. Austin. Mahwa: Paulist Press, 1980.
Kholi, Surindar Singh. *Sikh Ethics*. New Delhi: Munshiram Manoharlal Publishers,1996.
Loewe, R., ed. *Studies in Rationalism, Judaism and Universalism*. London: Humanities Press. 1966.
Novak, D. *Talking with Christians: Musings of a Jewish Theologian*. Grand Rapids, MI: Wm. B. Eerdmans, 2005.
Nesbitt, Eleanor. *Sikhism: A Very Short Introduction*. Oxford: Oxford University Press, 2005.
Puri, Shamsher Singh. *Handbook of Sikh Theology*. New Delhi: National Book Shop, 1999.
Radhakrishnan, Sarvepalli. *The Hindu Way of Life*. Indus, 1998.
Rambachan, Anantanand. *The Advaita Worldview: God, World and Humanity*. Albany: SUNY University Press, 2006.
Ratzinger, Joseph Cardinal. *Introductions to Christianity*. San Francisco: Ignatius Press, 1990.
Schacter, J. J., ed. *Judaism's Encounter with Other Cultures*. Northvale, NJ: Jason Aronson, 1997.
Scharen, Christian. *Faith as a Way of Life*. Grand Rapids, MI: Eerdmans, 2008.

Singh, Avtar. *Ethics of the Sikhs*. Patiala: Punjabi University, 1996.
Singh, Gurnam. "Sikhism's Emancipatory Discourses: Some critical perspectives." *Sikh Formations* 2 (December 2006).
Singh, Nirbahi. *Philosophy of Sikhism: Reality and its Manifestations*. New Delhi: Atlantic Publishers, 1990.
Singh, Wazir. *Sikhism: Philosophy and Culture*. New Delhi: National Book Shop, 1999.
Sharma, Arvind. *A Guide to Hindu Spirituality*. Bloomington, IN: World Wisdom Series, 2006.
Stevens, John. *Three Zen Masters: Ikkyu, Hakuin, and Ryokan*. Tokyo: Kodansha International, 1993.
Thich Nhat Hanh. *Being Peace*. Berkeley, CA: Parallax Press, 1987.
Tillich, Paul. *Systematic Theology*. Chicago: University of Chicago Press, 1963.
Tully, Mark. *India's Unending Journey*. London: Rider, 2008.
Volf, Miroslav. *Against the Tide: Love in a Time of Petty Dreams and Persisting Enmities*. Grand Rapids, MI: Eeardmans, 2010.
Volf, Miroslav. *Exclusion and Embrace. Theological Reflection on Identity, Otherness, and Reconciliation*. Nashville: Abingdon Press, 1996.
Welch, Holmes. *The Practice of Chinese Buddhism 1900–1950*. Cambridge, MA: Harvard University Press, 1967.
Wolffe, John, ed. *Religion in History: Conflict, Conversion, and Coexistence*. Manchester: Manchester University Press, 2004.

Index

acculturation, 10, 48, 55, 74, 85, 103
Advaita, 28
Akiva, Rabbi, 90, 93n19
Ananda, Venerable, 54, 60n10
Aristotle, 86
Auschwitz, 47
authenticity, xvii, 28, 68, 69, 72, 75, 85, 87, 99–100, 102–103
Avraham Ibn Ezra, Rabbi, 80, 93n8

Barth, Karl, 7
Bhagavadgita, 19, 20–21, 23–24, 26, 28–29
Bible (Christian)/Gospel, 2–3, 5, 10, 13, 68, 69, 70
brahmins, 22, 53

Cambodia, 59–60
caste, xvii, 22, 27, 49, 55
commercialization, 105–106
community, 25, 40, 70, 71, 79, 87, 99, 106, 110n8
compassion, 19–20, 30, 36, 38, 41, 42, 45, 46, 47, 49, 51, 52, 56, 57, 58, 60, 108
Confucianism, 48, 50
conversion. *See* proselytization

Dalai Lama, 49, 51, 58, 101
dalit (Buddhists), 55
Dharma, 45, 49, 52
diaspora, 85, 89
diversity, xiii, 4, 25, 26, 31, 96
Divine attributes, 30, 37, 42, 62, 64, 77, 98

ego. *See* humility
evangelism. *See* proselytization
Ezekiel, Prophet, 9

faith, xvii, 2, 7, 9, 10, 11, 12, 14n4, 21, 25, 39, 42, 104
faith communities, xi, xiii, xv, 5, 16n33, 21, 40, 44n3, 48, 55, 70, 72–73, 74, 87, 88, 98, 101, 104
forgiveness, xii, 11–13, 17n38, 28–31, 37, 42–43, 56, 63, 75–77, 90, 90–92

Gandhi, Mahatma, xviin3, 21, 26, 29, 51, 59, 101
Gaon of Vilna, 83
gender, xvii, 22, 27, 49
al-Ghazālī, Abū Hāmid, 64
globalization, xv, 4, 54–55, 72, 105, 106
Gobind, Guru, 38, 42
Granth, Guru/SGGS Ji, 34, 37, 38, 40, 41, 42, 44n5
Greek wisdom. *See* Hellenism

healing, 31, 47, 59, 90, 91
Hellenism, 3, 8, 10, 14n5, 15n23, 83, 84, 87, 89, 92n3, 93n9, 93n15, 102, 109n2
humility, 21, 25, 29, 34, 36, 38, 40, 42, 43, 67, 68, 75, 80, 104, 107–108, 108, 109

identity, xvi, 3, 9, 27, 28, 55, 85, 88, 102–103, 104, 109n4
ignorance, 20–21, 27, 29–30, 31, 58, 70
integrity, xvi, xvii, 8, 13, 85, 88, 99–100, 102, 109n4
intuition, 33, 34
Isaiah, Prophet, 7, 81

Jainism, xviin3, 11, 49
Jesus/Jesus Christ, 2, 3, 5, 6, 7, 9, 10, 12, 16n31, 24, 62, 68, 69
Joseph (Biblical prophet), 75–77
justice, 19, 27, 28, 50, 70, 76, 77, 90, 91
Justin Martyr, 10, 16n31

Ka'ba, 76
kalām, 71
Khmer Rouge. *See* Cambodia
King, Martin Luther, 59
Kook, Rabbi A.I., 83–84, 93n17, 99, 109

langar, 40
love/loving kindness, xii, 5, 11–12, 14, 28, 36, 37, 38, 39, 40, 41–42, 42, 45, 49, 56, 57–58, 60, 63–64, 64, 75, 76, 82, 84, 90–92, 93n15, 93n19, 108–109, 109n4, 111n52
Luqmān, Prophet, 62, 65, 67
Luther, Martin, 13, 17n40

Maimonides (Moses ben Maimon/Rambam), 81–82, 86, 92n5, 93n15
meditation. *See* prayer
mercy, 36, 42, 64, 65, 66, 68, 75, 76
mindfulness, 56
missionizing. *See* proselytization
Moses (Biblical prophet), 63, 65–66, 67, 68, 73, 75
Muhammad, Prophet, 5, 61, 63, 68, 75, 76, 77

Nanak, Guru, 34–35, 36, 37, 39, 40, 42
negative theology, 98
New Testament. *See* Bible

peace, xvi, xvii, 2, 56, 59, 84, 99
peacemaking, 13, 47, 59, 97, 99
prayer/meditation, 13, 17n38, 33, 35, 37, 39, 40, 42, 44n5, 47, 48, 49, 56, 60n12, 65, 82
proselytization, 7, 10, 17n34, 25, 104, 106
Proverbs (Bible), 2, 3, 80, 92n2

Qur'ān, 63, 64–65, 67, 67–70, 71–72, 73, 74, 75–76

Rabin, Yitchak, 59
Ramana Maharishi, 30
Rashi, 80, 93n8
respect, xv, xvi, xvii, 8–9, 10, 22, 23, 24, 47, 57, 65, 69, 72, 87, 90, 91, 92, 99, 103

Salafi movement, 72
Sarvodaya Shramadana, 47, 51
Al-Shahrastānī, Muhammad, 69, 72
Socrates, 8, 15n18
Soloveitchik, Joseph B. Rabbi, xviiin7, 88–89
Sri Lanka, 47
sunyata, 50
Sutta, Alagaddupama, 45–46

Talmud, 79, 81, 85, 89, 90, 91, 92n3, 92n4
Taoism, 48, 50
teacher/teacher-disciple, 34–35, 87, 88, 100–101
Thich Nhat Hanh, 49, 52
Tillich, Paul, 11, 16n32
Torah, 67, 68–69, 70, 79, 80, 81–82, 83, 90, 92n7, 93n15, 97
truth/truthful living, 3, 10, 16n31, 20, 21, 25, 27, 28, 28–30, 36, 38, 39, 43, 45, 46, 49, 52, 53, 54, 62, 65, 67, 67–68, 69–70, 72, 77, 80, 86, 90, 104, 108, 110n8
Tulasidasa, 19, 32n1

Upanishad, 21, 22, 23, 29

Veda, 20, 22, 26
Vilna Gaon. *See* Gaon of Vilna
Vivekananda, Swami, 24, 32n15

About the Contributors

Pal Ahluwalia's main research interests lie in the areas of African studies, social and cultural theory. He is a Fellow of the Academy of Social Sciences in Australia and was appointed to a UNESCO Chair in Transnational Diasporas and Reconciliation Studies in 2008. His latest book is *Out of Africa: Post-Structuralism's Colonial Roots* (2010). Professor Pal Ahluwalia presently serves as Pro Vice-Chancellor (Research and Innovation) at the Universality of Portsmouth.

Timothy J. Gianotti is an associate professor of Arabic & Islamic Studies at Renison University College, University of Waterloo (Canada). His publications include *Al-Ghazali's Unspeakable Doctrine of the Soul* (E. J. Brill, 2001), a study of controversies surrounding the soul and the afterlife within medieval Islamic philosophy, theology, and mysticism, and *In the Light of a Blessed Tree: Illuminations of Islamic Belief, Practice, and History* (Wipf & Stock, 2011), an experientially textured introduction to Islamic belief, practice, and history. His current work focuses on moral theology and spiritual formation within traditional Islamic frameworks, and he is a strong advocate for spiritual education both within and beyond the Muslim community.

Alon Goshen-Gottstein is acknowledged as one of the world's leading figures in interreligious dialogue, specializing in bridging the theological and academic dimension with a variety of practical initiatives, especially involving world religious leadership. He is both a theoretician and activist, setting trends and precedents in the global interfaith arena. He is the founder and director of the Elijah Interfaith Institute (formerly the Elijah School for the Study of Wisdom in World Religions), and its rich website is testimony to his many and varied activities. A noted scholar of Jewish studies, he has held academic posts at Tel Aviv University and has served as director of the Center for the Study of Rabbinic Thought, Beit Morasha College, Jerusalem. In addition to editing the *Interreligious Reflections* series, he has published several monographs and many articles. His most recent publications are *The Jewish Encounter with Hinduism: Wisdom, Spirituality Identity* and *Same God, Other god: Judaism, Hinduism and the Problem of Idolatry*, both published by Palgrave Macmillan, 2015.

Sallie B. King is Professor Emerita at James Madison University (Harrisonburg, VA) and Affiliate Faculty, Professor of Buddhist Studies, Department of Theology, Georgetown University (Washington, DC). She is author of *Socially Engaged Buddhism* and *Being Benevolence: The Social Ethics of Engaged Buddhism*, and co-editor (with Christopher S. Queen) of *Engaged Buddhism: Buddhist Liberation Movements in Asia*. She is the former president of the Society for Buddhist-Christian Studies and co-editor, with Paul O. Ingram, of *The Sound of Liberating Truth: Buddhist-Christian Dialogues in Honor of Frederick J. Streng*, which won the Frederick J. Streng Award for Excellence in Buddhist-Christian Studies.

Anantanand Rambachan is Professor of Religion, Philosophy and Asian Studies at Saint Olaf College, Minnesota. Prof. Rambachan is the author of numerous books, book-chapters and articles in scholarly journals. Prof. Rambachan has been involved in the field of interreligious relations and dialogue for over twenty-five years, as a Hindu participant and analyst. He has contributed to numerous consultations and discussions convened by national and international organizations concerned with interreligious issues. His latest book is *A Hindu Theology of Liberation: Not-Two is Not-One* (State University of New York Press, 2015)

Meir Sendor was the Rabbi of the Young Israel of Sharon, Massachusetts for three decades. A student of the late Rabbi Joseph B. Soloveitchik, he received his ordination from the Rabbi Isaac Elchanan Theological Seminary of Yeshiva University. He received his doctorate in Medieval Jewish History from Harvard University, under the late Professor Isadore Twersky. He teaches and writes on Jewish philosophy, Kabbalah, Hasidism, the philosophy of Jewish law, Jewish history, and Jewish ethics.

Miroslav Volf is the Founder and Director of Yale Center for Faith and Culture and Henry B. Wright Professor of Theology, Yale University Divinity School, New Haven, Connecticut. His most significant books include *Exclusion and Embrace* (1996; winner of Grawemeyer Award in Religion, and one of *Christianity Today*'s 100 most important religious books of the twentieth century), and *Flourishing: Why We Need Religion in a Globalized World* (2015). The main concern of his work is exploring resources of religious traditions for living flourishing lives in pluralistic, late capitalist societies.

www.ingramcontent.com/pod-product-compliance
Lightning Source LLC
Chambersburg PA
CBHW070920160426
43193CB00011B/1531